BROOKLYN BAR BITES

BROOKLYN BAR BITES

GREAT DISHES AND COCKTAILS FROM NEW YORK'S FOOD MECCA

BARBARA SCOTT-GOODMAN

Photography by Jennifer May

RIZZOLI
NEW YORK

New York Paris London Milan

CONTENTS

INTRODUCTION

There is a concept known as "the third place." It is not your home or your office, but another spot, a space that you visit run by someone else, one where you can be comfortable. Most often that place is a bar. In big cities, many people live and work in cramped apartments and offices, so they rely on their neighborhood bars, cafés, and eateries as that "third place" to unwind and have drinks, to meet and hang out with friends, to read, and to eat. Ideally the place has a warm atmosphere, good music, a welcoming bartender, and great food.

Great food at a bar? For years eating at the bar was almost a form of punishment. Bowls of salty peanuts or pretzels were the norm, served mainly to make you thirstier so you would order more drinks. But in recent years, there has been a food renaissance in bars that has gone hand in hand with the elevation and refinement of crafting cocktails. A number of diverse influences have inspired this movement—Spanish tapas bars, Japanese *izakayas,* British gastropubs, Southern roadhouses, and oyster bars, to name a few. Today bar owners, restaurateurs, and chefs are serving food at the bar with a new level of expertise and passion.

That brings us to Brooklyn, the New York borough that has become the epicenter of the latest culinary scene and a land of excellent bars that serve both classic and reinvented cocktails and amazing food. As the many neighborhoods that make up this vast borough change at warp speed, good local bars are springing up all over and ambitious cooks are creating and sending out an array of great snacks and dishes to accompany drinks.

Over the past few years, I have explored Brooklyn with friends and family in search of excellent food and cocktails, and I have been consistently impressed with the quality and inventiveness of the bar fare that's available. For example, Maison Premiere, a stylish Old-World spot in Williamsburg, serves pristine seafood, has a one-dollar oyster happy hour (as do many Brooklyn bars), and offers absinthe cocktails along with a superb selection of beer and wine. Dear Bushwick, a charming gastropub located in an industrial area of Bushwick, features scrumptious dishes that use locally sourced meat, fish, and produce, as well as original gin- and whiskey-based libations. Bar Chuko in Prospect Heights is an *izakaya* that serves fantastic small plates, rice bowls, and ramen to eat with flights of Japanese whiskey, sake, shochu, or innovative cocktails. And out on the waterfront of Red Hook, there is Fort Defiance, a modest bar and restaurant that offers high-quality drinks, oysters, and deceptively simple dishes like deviled eggs with fried capers. The roster of Brooklyn neighborhood bars and restaurants serving top-notch food and drinks goes on and on, so it is very easy to find a "third place" here. I am aware that I have only scratched the surface of this rich territory. Besides, bars and restaurants are always in a state of flux, with new spots opening, moving, or, sometimes, closing.

While it is true that today's Brooklyn is a bit of a scene, there is a wealth of genuinely good, thoughtful cooking going on in this lively borough. There are so many savvy, skilled, and energetic chefs creating delicious and innovative dishes made with well-sourced ingredients for diners to savor. The same goes for the many talented mixologists who are star players in Brooklyn bar culture. They take immense pride in their cocktail creations and well-chosen wine and beer selections.

With *Brooklyn Bar Bites,* I welcome all adventurous food enthusiasts, home cooks, and bartenders to join me on an exciting bar crawl through this wonderful, food-crazy mecca.

Cheers!

WILLIAMSBURG

Williamsburg is the quintessential neighborhood that typifies the "new Brooklyn." The area is a mash-up of old and new cultures that exist among old industrial buildings and warehouses, small single-family homes, and pricey new high-rises along the East River. It has long been a hub for creative young people, and it is prime territory for good music, shopping, and restaurant- and bar-hopping.

Rye
BAR

RYE

347 SOUTH FIRST STREET

Chef Cal Elliot has been a part of the Brooklyn culinary scene for years. After cooking stints at Gramercy Tavern and Blue Hill in Manhattan and at DuMont in Brooklyn, he decided to open his own place in rapidly gentrifying Williamsburg. Since Elliot had lived in the neighborhood since 1993, he felt that he truly understood the landscape, and he wanted to create a bar and restaurant that would serve his friends and neighbors well. In 2009 Elliot restored a turn-of-the-century factory, transforming it into the beautiful, elegant space that is now Rye. The delicious, satisfying food reflects the kitchen's talent and care, and the cocktails feature both classic and original libations meant to be savored in this warm, relaxing neighborhood spot.

GRILLED SCALLOP CEVICHE

In classic ceviche, the seafood "cooks" in a citrus bath before it is served, but if marinated too long, it will lose its firm consistency. To avoid this problem, the scallops for Rye's ceviche are quickly grilled, then drizzled with a citrus dressing—an excellent idea from a restaurant kitchen to yours.

SERVES 6 TO 8

Citrus Dressing:

3 jalapeño peppers, stemmed, seeded, and chopped

3 garlic cloves

1 tablespoon granulated sugar

1 cup fresh lime juice

1/2 cup fish sauce

3 tablespoons rice wine vinegar

3 tablespoons water

1 pound large sea scallops (about 10)

Kosher salt and freshly ground black pepper

Mixed greens, for serving

Sliced avocados, for serving

To make the dressing: Put the peppers, garlic, sugar, lime juice, fish sauce, vinegar, and water in a blender and blend until combined. Transfer to a nonreactive bowl, cover with plastic wrap, and refrigerate until ready to use.

Prepare a hot fire in a grill or heat a grill pan over medium-high heat (see Note).

Pat the scallops dry and season to taste with salt and black pepper. Grill the scallops until golden brown, 2 to 3 minutes per side.

Cut the scallops horizontally in half, transfer to the bowl of dressing, and gently toss together.

Arrange the greens and avocado slices on individual plates or a large platter. Spoon the scallops over them, drizzle with the remaining dressing, and serve.

Note: The scallops can also be pan-seared. Heat a tablespoon of olive oil in a large skillet over medium-high heat. Add the scallops and cook until golden brown, about 2 minutes per side.

DUCK RILLETTES

Rillettes ("ree-yet") are a potted meat made with duck, goose, or pork cooked in fat. Chef Elliot uses duck confit and blends in fresh goat cheese to create a very smooth version. Served with grilled bread, cornichons, and whole-grain mustard, his rillettes are a tasty appetizer or a delicious addition to a charcuterie board.

SERVES 6 TO 8

2 whole duck confit legs, with some of their fat

2 tablespoons whole-grain mustard

1 tablespoon finely chopped fresh thyme

1 tablespoon finely chopped fresh chives

1 garlic clove, roasted (see Note)

2 ounces fresh goat cheese, at room temperature

Kosher salt and freshly ground black pepper

Heat the duck legs in a large skillet over low heat until the fat melts. Remove the duck and strain. Pour ¼ cup of the fat into a bowl and refrigerate until well chilled. Reserve any remaining fat for another use.

Meanwhile, remove the duck meat from the bones. Discard the skin and bones, or save the bones for stock, if desired.

Put the duck meat, chilled duck fat, mustard, thyme, chives, and garlic in a food processor and process until the mixture comes together. Add the cheese and salt and pepper to taste and process again until smooth. Transfer the mixture to a ramekin and chill in the refrigerator for a few hours before serving.

The rillettes will keep, covered, in the refrigerator for up to a month.

Note: To make roasted garlic: Preheat the oven to 375°F. Line a baking dish with foil. Put 10 peeled garlic cloves in the center of the foil, drizzle with olive oil, and sprinkle with kosher salt. Fold up the edges of the foil and seal to make a packet. Bake until the garlic is softened and fragrant, about 45 minutes. Let cool.

BRUSSELS SPROUTS
WITH CREAMY GARLIC DRESSING

The trick to making these Brussels sprouts is to deep-fry them in a few inches of hot oil and remove them just as they begin to crisp, then toss them with dressing while they're still hot. The tangy dressing recipe makes a generous amount. That's not a bad thing—you'll want to have it on hand to serve with other vegetables and salads.

SERVES 6

Creamy Garlic Dressing:

5 large egg yolks

10 roasted garlic cloves (see Note, page 13)

2 anchovy fillets, chopped

1 tablespoon capers

¼ cup fresh lemon juice

¼ cup sherry vinegar

3 tablespoons whole-grain mustard

1 tablespoon Dijon mustard

2 teaspoons Worcestershire sauce

1 teaspoon Tabasco sauce

Kosher salt and freshly ground black pepper

1 cup extra-virgin olive oil

1 cup corn oil

2 cups heavy cream

8 strips bacon

Vegetable oil, for deep-frying

1 pound Brussels sprouts, trimmed and quartered

1 tablespoon capers

1 tablespoon chopped fresh flat-leaf parsley

½ cup freshly grated Parmesan cheese

Fresh lemon juice, for serving

To make the dressing: Put the egg yolks, garlic, anchovies, capers, lemon juice, vinegar, mustards, Worcestershire and Tabasco sauces, and salt and pepper to taste in a food processor and process until well blended. With the machine running, slowly add the oils through the feed tube in a steady stream, processing until incorporated. Add the heavy cream and process again. Taste and adjust the seasonings if necessary. The dressing will keep, covered, in the refrigerator for up to 2 weeks.

To make the Brussels sprouts: Fry the bacon in a large skillet over medium-high heat until quite crispy. Remove from the pan and drain on paper towels, then crumble when cool.

Pour 3 inches of vegetable oil into a deep heavy-bottomed pot and heat to 350°F over medium heat. Fry the Brussels sprouts until golden and just beginning to crisp, making sure that they don't burn.

Using a skimmer or a slotted spoon, transfer the Brussels sprouts to a large bowl. Working quickly, add 2 tablespoons of the dressing, the bacon, capers, and parsley and toss together. Sprinkle with the cheese, drizzle fresh lemon juice and serve.

BASIC BAR EQUIPMENT

You don't need a lot of specialized equipment to mix good drinks, but you do need a few basics to outfit a home bar. Aside from common kitchen utensils—a bottle opener, a can opener, and a corkscrew—here are a few tools that you will need.

Boston Shaker: A Boston shaker is composed of two tumblers: a 24-ounce metal tumbler and a 16-ounce mixing glass. The metal shaker fits around the rim of the mixing glass to form an airtight seal for making shaken cocktails. Most cocktails are built in the mixing glass, since it is transparent and you can see how much liquid is being added.

Cobbler Shaker: A cobbler shaker is usually stainless steel. It has a base shaker and a snug-fitting top with a built-in strainer.

Hawthorn Strainer: This strainer is used with a Boston shaker to strain ice from cocktails. It has a metal coil on its underside and it fits easily within the metal shaker lid.

Julep Strainer: This strainer looks like a large perforated spoon and is so named because it is used to keep pieces of mint out of juleps. It is also used for straining all types of cocktails made in a mixing glass.

Jigger: The classic jigger is two adjoined stainless steel cones in sizes ranging from ½ to 2½ ounces.

Bar Spoon: This 12-inch-long spoon with a twisted spiral handle is used both for stirring and as a measuring device.

Muddler: Muddlers are used to crush fruits, herbs, and sugar. The best muddlers are made of wood and are generally 6 to 8 inches long with a flat side on one side.

Paring Knife: Paring knives usually have a 4-inch blade that tapers to a fine point. They are used for cutting lemons, limes, and oranges for garnishes.

Channel Zester: This zester has a rounded or rectangular metal head with a small curved blade and a hole on one side or the top. It is used for making long citrus-peel swirls.

Citrus Zester: This is a small hand tool with tiny holes at the end of what looks like a palette knife. It is used to make small threads of zest.

Spice Grater: This is used to grate nutmeg and other spices over poured cocktails. A Microplane works just as well and is easy to clean.

SOUTHSIDE

SERVES 1

¼ cup peeled and chopped
   cucumber, plus a thin slice
   of cucumber for garnish

5 fresh mint leaves

2 ounces Gordon's gin

¾ ounce Simple Syrup
   (recipe follows)

½ ounce fresh lime juice

Club soda

Muddle the chopped cucumber and mint leaves in the bottom of a cocktail shaker. Fill the shaker with ice and add the gin, simple syrup, and lime juice. Shake well and double-strain into a highball glass. Add ice and top off with club soda. Garnish with the cucumber slice and serve.

SIMPLE SYRUP

MAKES ABOUT 1½ CUPS

2 cups granulated sugar

1 cup water

Simple syrup is a mixture of sugar and water, and is an important element to all manner of drinks. It is very easy to prepare and is always good to have on hand.

Combine the sugar and water in a medium heavy-bottomed saucepan and bring to a gentle boil over medium-high heat, stirring to dissolve the sugar. Reduce the heat and simmer until the sugar is completely dissolved and the syrup is slightly thickened, about 3 minutes. Remove from the heat and let cool.

Transfer the syrup to a clean container with a lid, cover, and refrigerate until ready to use. Simple syrup will keep in the refrigerator for up to a month.

CLASSIC OLD-FASHIONED

SERVES 1

2 ounces Old Overholt rye

1 bar spoon Demerara Simple Syrup
  (recipe follows)

2 dashes orange bitters

2 dashes Angostura bitters

1 lemon twist, for garnish

Demerara Simple Syrup:

1 cup Demerara sugar

1 cup water

Fill a mixing glass halfway with ice. Add the rye, syrup, and bitters, stir well, and strain into a rocks glass with one large ice cube. Garnish with the lemon twist and serve.

To make the Demerara Simple Syrup: Combine the sugar and water in a small saucepan and bring to a boil over medium heat. Then reduce the heat to low and simmer for 15 minutes. Let cool.

Transfer the syrup to a clean container with a lid. It will keep, covered, in the refrigerator, for 5 days.

MAISON PREMIERE

298 BEDFORD AVENUE

Inspired by Old-World drinking establishments in New Orleans, Maison Premiere is a stylish oyster house and cocktail den that offers a unique drinking and dining experience. The decor includes details such as copper oyster tubs, yellow pine floor-boards, and vintage hardware throughout the restaurant. The knowledgeable staff welcomes guests with warm hospitality. Over thirty different varieties of East and West Coast oysters are on the menu, along with the largest selection of premium absinthes in the city. This beautiful spot has been wildly popular since it opened in 2011; and customers line up at the door every late afternoon to take advantage of its $1.00 oyster happy hour.

PICKLED OYSTERS

Chef Lisa Giffen makes pickled oysters with seasonal vegetables, like fresh peppers and green beans in the summer and cauliflower and fennel in late fall and winter. They are a great bar snack and a good accompaniment to a dry martini.

MAKES ABOUT 1 QUART

Pickling Spice:

1 teaspoon black peppercorns

1 teaspoon coriander seeds

½ teaspoon red pepper flakes

1 bay leaf

1 cinnamon stick, broken into 4 pieces

1 whole clove

½ cup packed brown sugar

¼ cup kosher salt

2 cups white wine vinegar

½ cup water

2 tablespoons Worcestershire sauce

1 teaspoon mustard seeds

Oysters:

30 large, meaty East Coast oysters, such as Blue Points, shucked

1 lemon, thinly sliced

1 white onion, thinly sliced

To make the pickling spice: Put the peppercorns, coriander, red pepper flakes, bay leaf, and cinnamon stick in a small bowl and stir together. Transfer to a large saucepan and add the brown sugar, salt, vinegar, water, Worcestershire sauce, and mustard seeds. Bring to a boil and cook, stirring occasionally, until the salt and sugar dissolve. Set aside.

Bring a pot of salted water to a boil. Add the oysters and cook for 1 minute; drain.

Layer the oysters, lemon, and onion in a large clean jar with a lid. Pour the pickling liquid over them. Cover and refrigerate overnight before serving.

The oysters will keep, covered, in the refrigerator for up to a month.

ASPARAGUS, MORELS & POACHED OYSTERS

Maison Premiere showcases this recipe every spring and serves it with a puree of fresh peas. The grassiness of the asparagus and earthiness of the morels go perfectly with salty Blue Point oysters, which become very sweet and succulent when lightly poached.

SERVES 6

1 pound morels

2 tablespoons olive oil, plus more for serving

4 shallots or 1 white onion, finely diced

4 tablespoons unsalted butter

1 cup dry white wine, such as Muscadet or Chardonnay

4 cups chicken or vegetable stock

Sea salt

2 pounds large asparagus, trimmed

12 large oysters, such as Blue Points, shucked and drained

2 lemons, seeded, segmented, and diced

The day before serving, clean the morels by washing them in five changes of lukewarm water. Drain thoroughly in a colander and lay them on a tray lined with paper towels. Refrigerate overnight.

Heat the olive oil in a small pot over medium heat. Add the shallots and sauté until translucent, 4 to 5 minutes. Add the butter and cook until it begins to foam. Add the morels and cook, stirring, for 8 minutes. Add the wine, stirring to deglaze the pot; then cook until reduced by half.

Add the stock and bring to a boil, then reduce the heat and simmer, partially covered, for 35 minutes.

Meanwhile, fill a large skillet with water, add a generous amount of salt, and bring to a boil. Blanch the asparagus for 2 minutes; drain. Arrange on warmed plates, drizzle with olive oil, and sprinkle with salt. Keep warm.

Bring the morel mixture to a light boil. Add the oysters and cook over medium-low heat, stirring occasionally, until they plump up, about 4 minutes. Stir in the lemon.

Spoon the morels, oysters, and sauce evenly over the asparagus and serve.

ADONIS

SERVES 1

3 dashes orange bitters

1½ ounces Carpano Antica vermouth

1 ounce Oloroso sherry

¾ ounce Pedro Ximénez sherry

1 long lemon twist, for garnish

Fill a mixing glass with ice. Add the bitters, vermouth, and the sherries and stir with a bar spoon. Strain into a long-stemmed coupe filled with ice. Garnish with the lemon twist and serve.

WOLCOTT EXPRESS

SERVES 1

1 teaspoon crème de menthe

½ ounce Kübler absinthe

¾ ounce fresh lime juice

¾ ounce lime cordial

1½ ounces Génépy liqueur

A fistful of mint sprigs

Fill a cocktail shaker with ice. Add the crème de menthe, absinthe, lime juice, lime cordial, liqueur, and mint and shake vigorously. Strain into a long-stemmed coupe over one large ice cube and serve.

OYSTERS

Long before New York City was known for pizza, hot dogs, or bagels, the oyster was considered its iconic food. From the 1700s to the 1800s, oyster beds were abundant in New York Harbor. Oysters were consumed by the upper classes in oyster bars and fine restaurants and could be bought on the cheap from street carts as well. Sadly, the oyster population declined in the early 1900s because of pollution and overfishing, and the industry disappeared.

Today, oysters sourced from the East and West coasts are wildly popular and served at many restaurants and bars throughout Brooklyn. A number of places host happy hours where customers can slurp $1.00 oysters along with beer, wine, or cocktails.

Here is a selection of excellent oysters from both coasts of the United States and Canada. Some of their names—Blue Pool, East Beach Blonde, Montauk Pearl—are as enticing as their flavors.

WEST COAST
CANADA & UNITED STATES

BRITISH COLUMBIA

Chefs Creek –
  mild brininess, sweet flavor, sweet finish
Fanny Bay –
  mild brininess, clean flavor, cucumber finish
Kusshi –
  mild brininess; clean, delicate flavor; fruity finish
Malaspina –
  mild brininess, sweet flavor, watermelon finish
Nootka Sound –
  high brininess; sweet, nutty flavor; anise finish
Stellar Bay –
  mild brininess, delicate flavor, clean finish

WASHINGTON STATE

Blue Pool –
  high brininess, earthy flavor, mineral finish
Chelsea Gem –
  low brininess, sweet flavor, creamy finish
Hama Hama –
  mild brininess; clean, crisp flavor; fruity finish
Kumamoto –
  mild brininess, sweet flavor, melon finish
Naked Roy's Beach –
  mild brininess; rich, sweet flavor; fruity finish
Olympia –
  high brininess, sweet flavor, coppery finish
Penn Cove –
  high brininess, sweet flavor, cucumber finish

Skookum or Little Skookum –
low brininess, full flavor, vegetable finish
Totten Inlet –
mild brininess; complex, full flavor; seaweed finish
Westcott Bay –
mild brininess, sweet flavor, mineral finish

OREGON

Willapa Bay –
high brininess, sweet flavor, cucumber finish

CALIFORNIA

Hog Island Sweetwaters –
light brininess, sweet flavor, smoky finish

EAST COAST
CANADA & UNITED STATES

PRINCE EDWARD ISLAND

Colville Bay –
mild brininess, clean flavor, sweet finish

Cooke's Cove Malpeque –
high brininess, crisp flavor, clean finish

NEW BRUNSWICK

Beausoleil –
mild brininess, clean flavor, sweet finish

La St. Simon –
medium brininess, sweet flavor, citrus finish

NOVA SCOTIA

Alba Bras D'Or –
high brininess; delicate, sweet flavor; musky finish

MAINE

Belon –
mild brininess, coppery flavor, mineral finish
Glidden Point –
high brininess; sweet, crisp flavor; mineral finish

MASSACHUSETTS

Cuttyhunk –
high brininess; light, clean flavor; mineral finish
Duxbury –
high brininess, buttery flavor, sweet finish
Island Creek –
high brininess; sweet, buttery flavor; mossy finish
Wellfleet –
high brininess; sweet flavor; crisp, clean finish
Wianno –
high brininess, sweet flavor, seaweed finish

RHODE ISLAND

East Beach Blonde –
medium brininess, mild flavor, mineral finish
Moonstone –
high brininess; rich, umami flavor; mineral finish
Watch Hill –
high brininess; rich flavor; buttery, sweet finish

NEW YORK/CONNECTICUT

Blue Point –
high brininess, mild flavor, sweet finish
Montauk Pearl –
high brininess; sweet, crisp flavor; melon finish
Oysterponds –
high brininess; strong, savory flavor; metallic finish

CHESAPEAKE BAY

Chincoteague –
high brininess, salty flavor, sweet finish
Rappahannock River –
mild brininess, sweet flavor, clean finish

GULF COAST

Apalachicola Bay –
mild brininess, clean taste, seaweed fiinish

THE RICHARDSON

451 GRAHAM AVENUE

Simply put, The Richardson is a proper American bar whose motto is "Not done fancy, just done right." Located on the Williamsburg/Greenpoint border, this handsome spot offers expertly crafted classic and house cocktails, and it also has an excellent selection of draft beers and a well-curated wine list of reds, whites, pinks, and bubblies. The kitchen serves delicious bar snacks such as fish platters, cheese and charcuterie plates, and sandwiches all day and night, and well into the wee hours of the morning.

GIN-CURED GRAVLAX

One of the specialties at The Richardson is a fish platter loaded with briny treats including gravlax, a salmon fillet that is cured with gin, lime, and juniper berries. The sweet-and-salty elements give this dish a distinctive flavor. Serve it with cream cheese, sliced red onions, and capers, along with bagels or black bread, or chop it into a salmon tartare. Be sure to allow enough time—3 days—for the salmon to cure.

SERVES 6 TO 8

½ cup kosher salt

½ cup packed brown sugar, plus 1 tablespoon

Grated zest of 1 lime

2 tablespoons freshly ground black pepper

One 1½-pound skin-on fresh salmon fillet

¼ cup City of London dry gin

1 tablespoon crushed juniper berries (use the side of a heavy knife)

Stir the salt, sugar, lime zest, and pepper together in a small bowl and mix with your fingers until well blended.

Put the salmon fillet, skin side up, on a large sheet of plastic wrap on a rimmed baking sheet. Pour half the gin evenly over the salmon. Spread half the salt mixture over the skin, then carefully flip the salmon over. Pour the rest of the gin over the salmon and rub with the remaining salt mixture. Spread the juniper berries over the salmon, pressing lightly so they won't fall off.

Wrap the salmon in the plastic wrap, then double-wrap with a second sheet of plastic wrap. Put it on a platter, cover with another platter, and put a 4- or 5-pound weight on top. Put the salmon in the refrigerator for 3 days and turn it over once a day.

When ready to serve, unwrap the salmon and transfer it to a cutting board. Using a long, thin, sharp knife, cut the salmon into thin slices at a 30-degree angle. The traditional cut starts diagonally at one corner of the salmon, then works back toward the center of the fillet. Discard the skin. Arrange the salmon slices on a platter and serve.

SMOKED BLUEFISH PÂTÉ

This creamy, smoky spread is great served with sliced cucumbers and grilled black bread. The bar's kitchen usually prepares the pâté with smoked bluefish, but it's also very tasty made with smoked trout or salmon.

MAKES ABOUT 1½ CUPS

8 ounces smoked bluefish fillet
(see Note)

8 ounces cream cheese, softened

1 tablespoon olive oil

3 tablespoons fresh lemon juice

1 tablespoon Worcestershire sauce

2 or 3 dashes Tabasco sauce

Pinch of cayenne pepper

Freshly ground black pepper

Toast, grilled bread, or crackers,
for serving

With a sharp knife, remove the skin and blood line (the very dark, soft parts in the middle of the fillet near the skin) from the bluefish, if necessary, and discard. Flake the fish with a fork, and set aside.

Put the cream cheese, olive oil, lemon juice, Worcestershire and Tabasco sauces, and cayenne pepper in a food processor and pulse until blended. Add the fish and pulse quickly for a chunky mixture, or pulse a bit longer for a smoother puree. Add black pepper to taste.

Serve the pâté with toast, grilled bread, or crackers.

Note: Smoked bluefish is available at fish markets and specialty stores.

SCOTTISH DEW

SERVES 1

6 thin cucumber slices

½ bar spoon superfine sugar

4 dashes Regan's orange bitters

¼ ounce Luxardo maraschino
liqueur

1¾ ounces blended Scotch

Muddle 4 cucumber slices, the sugar, and the bitters together in a large mixing glass. Add the liqueur, Scotch, and ice, cover, and shake. Pour into a double rocks glass filled with ice, garnish with the remaining 2 cucumber slices, and serve.

GINGER LEE #2

SERVES 1

½ ounce fresh lemon juice

½ ounce P&H ginger syrup

2 ounces Zaya 12-year Trinidadian rum

4 dashes Regan's orange bitters

Fill a cocktail shaker with ice. Add the lemon juice, ginger syrup, rum, and bitters and shake vigorously. Strain into a chilled cocktail glass and serve.

THE NOBLE EXPERIMENT

Bridget Firtle established The Noble Experiment in Bushwick in 2011. After a career in finance and analyzing publicly traded alcohol companies, Firtle, a born-and-bred New Yorker, pursued her dream of having her own business. With her life savings and supportive investors, she founded The Noble Experiment, whose name is a euphemism for Prohibition. The distillery produces Owney's rum, a dry white rum that is made in small batches using top-grade GMO-free domestic molasses, yeast, and New York City tap water. Owney's is named after Owen "Owney" Madden, a legendary Prohibition-era gangster and bootlegger who ran rum from the Caribbean to the shores of the Rockaways. He also made handsome profits from his speakeasies and nightclubs, including the famed Cotton Club in Harlem. Owney's rum is smooth and substantial and has a delicately sweet aftertaste with notes of citrus and spice. Because of its unique flavor, Owney's is a top choice among bartenders for classic daiquiris, tiki drinks, and other specialty rum cocktails.

The Noble Experiment offers self-guided and distiller-hosted tours, and guests are welcome at the onsite distillery-bar.

THE NOBLE EXPERIMENT, 23 Meadow Street, Brooklyn, NY 11206, www.owneys.com

BLACK WING

SERVES 1

Ginger beer

1¾ ounces Cruzan Black Strap rum

¼ ounce Fernet Branca bitters

Fill a Collins glass with ice. Add ginger beer until it is three-quarters full. Insert a straw in the glass and slowly pour the rum over the ice so the rum sits on top of the ginger beer. Float the bitters on top and serve.

GRAND ꝰ FERRY

GRAND FERRY TAVERN

229 KENT AVENUE

Grand Ferry, a nautical-themed waterfront tavern near the East River, is The Richardson's sister restaurant. It has a similar look and vibe—warm, dark wood; printed damask wallpaper; antique chandeliers; and a killer playlist that ranges from rockabilly to cool jazz—and serves proper cocktails, as well as beer and wine. In addition to its extensive raw bar, Grand Ferry offers tasty seafood dishes like clam chowder, clams casino, and fried oyster rolls. Hearty updated bar classics such as wild mushroom shepherd's pie and grass-fed burgers are also on the menu.

BROOKLYN CLAM CHOWDER

According to food historians, Manhattan clam chowder was once scorned by New Englanders, who felt that only people who lived in New York City would be crazy enough to add tomatoes to their beloved soup—hence the name. Grand Ferry Tavern ladles out its own delicious Brooklyn-style rendition—loaded with fresh local littleneck clams and Yukon Gold potatoes— and no one thinks it's crazy at all.

SERVES 6

2 tablespoons vegetable oil

1 onion, finely chopped

2 garlic cloves, minced

2 leeks, rinsed, drained, and finely chopped

2 carrots, peeled and diced

2 celery stalks, diced

1 fennel bulb, trimmed and diced

Pinch of paprika

Pinch of cayenne pepper

Pinch of red pepper flakes

1 bay leaf, 1 sprig thyme, and 2 sprigs parsley, tied together to make a bouquet garni

Kosher salt and freshly ground black pepper

2 tablespoons unsalted butter

1 tablespoon all-purpose flour

¾ cup dry white wine

Dash of Sriracha sauce

Dash of Worcestershire sauce

1 cup tomato juice

¾ cup bottled clam juice

4 cups water or vegetable or fish stock, or as needed

2 cups cubed unpeeled Yukon Gold potatoes

2 dozen littleneck clams, rinsed

Olive oil, for serving

Chopped fresh flat-leaf parsley, for garnish

Heat the vegetable oil in a stockpot or Dutch oven over medium heat. Add the onion and sauté until translucent. Add the garlic, leeks, carrots, celery, and fennel and cook until softened but not browned. Add the paprika, cayenne pepper, red pepper flakes, bouquet garni, and salt and pepper to taste and cook, stirring, for 5 minutes.

Remove the bouquet garni from the pot. Add the butter and stir until it melts. Add the flour and cook, stirring, to form a roux; do not let it color. Add ¼ cup of the white wine and cook,

stirring, until reduced by half. Add the Sriracha and Worcestershire sauces and the tomato and clam juices and cook for 10 minutes.

Add the water and bring to a boil. Reduce the heat to maintain a simmer, add the potatoes, cover, and simmer, stirring and skimming off the foam occasionally, until the potatoes are tender, about 20 minutes. Add more water if the chowder seems too thick. Taste and adjust the seasonings if necessary.

Meanwhile, put the remaining ½ cup wine and the clams in a large pot. Bring to a boil, cover, and cook just until the clams open. Remove the clams with a slotted spoon. Discard any unopened clams.

Ladle the chowder into shallow soup bowls and arrange the clams in the centers of the bowls, Drizzle each serving with olive oil, garnish with parsley, and serve.

THE PEACEMAKER

The Peacemaker got its name from a common turn-of-the-century term, "peace offering." When gents would return home after a long night of carousing, they would bring along a hoagie roll stuffed with delicious fried oysters for their wives. Here is an adaptation of Grand Ferry's recipe, made with a toasted brioche roll and slathered with spicy rémoulade sauce.

SERVES 6

Spicy Rémoulade Sauce:

1½ cups mayonnaise

¼ cup whole-grain mustard

1 garlic clove, minced

1 tablespoon pickle juice

1 tablespoon drained capers

1 teaspoon horseradish

¼ teaspoon cayenne pepper

¼ teaspoon hot paprika

½ teaspoon Cholula or other hot sauce

1 cup buttermilk

Kosher salt and freshly ground black pepper

48 oysters, shucked and drained

1 cup all-purpose flour

½ cup cornmeal

½ cup plain bread crumbs

2 tablespoons Old Bay seasoning

Vegetable oil, for deep-frying

6 brioche or potato hot dog rolls, split, toasted if desired

Chopped fresh flat-leaf parsley, for garnish

Lemon wedges, for serving

To make the spicy rémoulade sauce: Put the mayonnaise, mustard, garlic, pickle juice, capers, horseradish, cayenne pepper, paprika, and hot sauce in a bowl and stir to combine. Taste and adjust the seasonings if necessary. Refrigerate until ready to serve.

Mix the buttermilk and salt and pepper to taste together in a medium bowl. Add the oysters and let stand for 5 minutes. Meanwhile, mix the flour, cornmeal, bread crumbs, and Old Bay together in a shallow bowl.

Pour 3 inches of oil into a deep heavy-bottomed pot and heat to 350°F over medium-high heat. Dredge the oysters in the flour mixture, shaking off any excess. Working in batches, fry the oysters until golden brown and crisp, 2 to 3 minutes, drain on paper towels.

Stuff the rolls with the oysters, spoon some of the sauce over the oysters, and garnish with parsley. Serve with additional sauce and lemon wedges.

VEGETABLE SHEPHERD'S PIE
WITH MUSHROOM SAUCE

Made with layered sautéed vegetables, greens, mushrooms, and mashed potatoes and served with a mushroom sauce, this is a heavenly version of shepherd's pie. It can be prepared as a vegan dish by mashing the potatoes with olive oil, or you can go the traditional route by adding butter and cream.

SERVES 8
SPECIAL EQUIPMENT: EIGHT 4- TO 5-INCH DIAMETER RING MOLDS

3 tablespoons olive oil

2 cups peeled and finely chopped carrots

2 cups peeled and finely chopped butternut or acorn squash

2 cups peeled and finely chopped zucchini

1 cup fresh corn kernels

1 cup fresh or frozen peas

Kosher salt and freshly ground black pepper

1 garlic clove, minced

1 small bunch kale or Swiss chard, trimmed, stemmed, and coarsely chopped

Mashed Potatoes:

6 to 8 large potatoes, peeled and cubed

4 garlic cloves

Kosher salt

1/4 cup olive oil

1 tablespoon unsalted butter (optional)

2 tablespoons heavy cream (optional)

Mushroom Sauce:

2 tablespoons olive oil

1 large onion, finely chopped

1 garlic clove, finely minced

1 medium carrot, finely chopped

1 celery stalk, chopped

4 cups mixed mushrooms, such as white button, cremini, and/or shiitake

Kosher salt and freshly ground black pepper

2 tablespoons dry white wine

1 tablespoon sherry vinegar

Sprigs of fresh parsley, thyme, rosemary, and oregano, tied together to make a bouquet garni

1 cup water

Sea salt, preferably Maldon

1/2 cup chopped mixed fresh herbs, such as flat-leaf parsley, thyme, rosemary, and oregano

Heat 2 tablespoons of the olive oil in a large skillet over medium heat. Add the carrots and butternut squash and cook, stirring occasionally, for 10 minutes. Add the zucchini, corn, and peas and cook until all the vegetables are tender, 10 to 15 minutes. Add salt and pepper to taste and set aside.

Heat the remaining 1 tablespoon olive oil in another skillet over medium heat. Add the garlic and cook until softened, about 2 minutes. Add the kale and salt and pepper to taste and cook, tossing with tongs, until the kale is wilted. Drain the kale well, squeeze, and wrap in a kitchen towel to remove excess liquid. Set aside.

To make the mashed potatoes: Rinse the potatoes in a colander under cold water until the water runs clear. Put them in a large pot with the garlic and salt to taste and add cold water to cover by 1 inch. Bring to a boil, then reduce the heat and simmer until the potatoes are tender but not mushy, about 15 minutes. Drain in a colander set over another pot or bowl; reserve the cooking water.

Transfer the potatoes to a stand mixer fitted with the whisk attachment and mix until smooth. Stop and scrape down the sides with a rubber spatula. With the mixer on low speed, add the olive oil and enough of the cooking water to make a very smooth puree. The potatoes can also be mashed by hand with a potato masher. Taste and adjust the seasonings if necessary. The mash can be finished with the butter and cream, if desired. Set aside.

To make the mushroom sauce: Heat the olive oil in a large skillet over medium-high heat. Add the onion, garlic, carrot, and celery and cook until just softened, about 5 minutes. Add the mushrooms and salt and pepper to taste and cook until the mushrooms begin to brown. Add the wine, vinegar, and bouquet garni and cook until reduced by half. Add the water and simmer until reduced by half. Taste and adjust the seasonings if necessary. Remove the bouquet garni and drain the mushrooms and vegetables in a sieve set over a saucepan, then transfer the mushrooms to a bowl. Cover the sauce to keep warm.

Preheat the broiler. Arrange the ring molds in the centers of 8 flameproof plates. Layer the kale, mushrooms, and sautéed vegetables in the molds. Top with mashed potatoes. Broil until the top of the potatoes is nicely browned.

Remove the ring molds. These will be very hot, so remove with tongs. Spoon the mushroom sauce over the pies, sprinkle with sea salt and the herbs, and serve.

TOKYO FIR

SERVES 1

¼ ounce fresh lemon juice

¼ ounce P&H ginger syrup

¼ ounce Dolin sweet vermouth

½ ounce Zirbenz Stone Pine liqueur

1¾ ounces Ransom Old Tom gin

1 lemon twist, for garnish

Fill a cocktail shaker with ice. Add the lemon juice, ginger syrup, vermouth, liqueur, and gin and shake vigorously. Strain into a chilled cocktail glass. Garnish with the lemon twist and serve.

BROOKLYN SPIRITS

NEW YORK DISTILLING COMPANY

New York Distilling Company was cofounded in 2011 by Brooklyn Brewery alum Tom Potter, his son Bill, and spirits business consultant Allen Katz. They currently produce three varieties of flavorful gin—Dorothy Parker, Perry's Tot, and Chief Gowanus—in their Williamsburg distillery. Their spirits are widely used in bars and restaurants all over the city. The Shanty, a full-service bar, is next door. It features cocktails, crafted by head bartender Nate Dumas, made with New York Distilling Company's spirits and others from all over the world. A selection of craft brews is also available.

New York Distilling Company is open for tours and tastings on weekends.

NEW YORK DISTILLING COMPANY, 79 Richardson Street, Brooklyn, NY 11211, www.nydistilling.com

SINGANI SPRITZ

SERVES 1

½ ounce fresh grapefruit juice

½ ounce Aperol Aperitivo liquor

1 ounce Singani 63 brandy

Sparkling rosé, such as Juve y Camps
   Pinot Noir rosé cava

1 orange twist, for garnish

Fill a cocktail shaker with ice. Add the grapefruit juice, Aperol, and brandy and shake vigorously. Strain into a wineglass, add ice, and top off with sparkling rosé. Garnish with the orange twist and serve.

NAKED CONDESSA

SERVES 1

¼ ounce grenadine

¼ ounce Cholula
   or other hot pepper sauce

½ ounce fresh orange juice

½ ounce fresh lime juice

1½ ounces Fortaleza blanco tequilla

Fill a cocktail shaker with ice. Add the grenadine, hot sauce, orange and lime juices, and tequila and shake vigorously. Strain into a cocktail glass and serve.

HOTEL DELMANO

82 BERRY STREET

Hotel Delmano has the aura of a romantic speakeasy from the 1920s. Whether you take a seat at the long, curving marble bar or in one of the plush dark back rooms, you are sure to enjoy a well-crafted drink from its seasonal cocktail menu, which includes a sherry-based drink called Ghost Dance and Ninety-Nine Roses made with gin, pear liqueur, and rose water. This opulent place features a raw bar that serves pristine seafood, and it also offers cheese and charcuterie boards and other small plates that pair beautifully with cocktails and wine.

ROASTED ROSEMARY NUTS

These simple roasted nuts are delicious to nibble on with drinks. Prepare this salty, crunchy snack made with fresh herbs as your go-to party dish.

MAKES 4 CUPS

4 cups mixed nuts, such as almonds, pecans, walnuts, and cashews

2 tablespoons olive oil

2 teaspoons kosher salt, plus more to taste

4 fresh rosemary sprigs, chopped

2 fresh thyme sprigs, chopped, plus more for garnish

Freshly ground black pepper

Preheat the oven to 250°F.

Put the nuts in a large bowl; add the olive oil, salt, rosemary, and thyme; and toss well to coat evenly.

Spread the nuts in a single layer on a rimmed baking sheet and roast, shaking the pan occasionally, until the coating is dry and the nuts are lightly browned and fragrant, 25 to 30 minutes.

Remove from the oven, sprinkle the nuts with additional salt and pepper to taste, and let cool, 10 to 15 minutes. (The nuts will keep in an airtight container for up to 1 week.) To serve, garnish the nuts with thyme leaves.

SEAFOOD SAUCES

Hotel Delmano serves an impressive array of seafood at the bar, from icy trays of raw oysters to seafood towers piled high with fresh clams, shrimp, crab, and caviar. They are served with a variety of house-made sauces to accompany and enhance these fresh bites from the sea.

COCKTAIL SAUCE

MAKES ABOUT 1 CUP

1 cup ketchup

2 tablespoon grated fresh horseradish

1 teaspoon Worcestershire sauce

1 tablespoon fresh lime juice,
   plus more as needed

1 tablespoon fresh orange juice

Dash of habanero hot sauce

Put the ketchup, horseradish, Worcestershire sauce, lime and orange juices, and hot sauce in a bowl and stir to combine. Taste and adjust the seasonings if necessary. Chill the sauce in the refrigerator for a few hours before serving.

MIGNONETTE SAUCE

MAKES ABOUT 3/4 CUP

1/4 cup red wine vinegar

1/4 cup sherry vinegar

2 tablespoons finely minced shallots

Kosher salt and freshly ground black pepper

Put the red wine and sherry vinegars, shallots, and salt and pepper to taste in a bowl and whisk together. Add a bit of water, if necessary. Chill the sauce in the refrigerator for a few hours before serving.

HOTEL DELMANO SAUCE

MAKES ABOUT ¾ CUP

¼ cup finely diced onion

¼ cup finely diced celery

¼ cup finely diced plum tomato

1 tablespoon fresh lemon juice, plus more as needed

1 tablespoon chopped fresh cilantro

Kosher salt and freshly ground black pepper

Put the onion, celery, tomato, lemon juice, cilantro, and salt and pepper to taste in a bowl and stir to combine. Add more lemon juice if the mixture seems too thick. Chill the sauce in the refrigerator for a few hours before serving.

NINETY-NINE ROSES

SERVES 1

1½ ounces Gordon's gin
½ ounce Rothman & Winter pear liqueur
¾ ounce fresh lemon juice
½ ounce Ginger Simple Syrup (see below)
Rose water, for spraying
1 lemon twist, for garnish

Fill a cocktail shaker with ice. Add the gin, pear liqueur, lemon juice, and ginger syrup, and shake well. Strain into a coupe and, using an atomizer, spray rose water on top of the drink. Garnish with the lemon twist and serve.

To make the Ginger Simple Syrup: Follow the Simple Syrup recipe (on page 16). Add four 1-inch pieces of trimmed and peeled fresh ginger to the sugar and water mixture and cook according to directions. Let cool and strain into a clean container with a lid, cover, and refrigerate until ready to use.

GREENPOINT

Greenpoint is the northernmost neighborhood of Brooklyn. It's home to a large Polish population and a mix of families and young professionals who enjoy its small-town charm and cozy vibe, along with beautiful views of the Manhattan skyline.

LITTLE DOKEBI

85 DRIGGS AVENUE

Little Dokebi is the sister restaurant to Dokebi Bar & Grill, a long-established Korean spot in Williamsburg that is owned and operated by Chul Kim. In 2013, he expanded to Greenpoint and opened this little gem of a bar, which has a cozy, woodsy interior and a very relaxed vibe. The menu includes Korean street food, such as Korean fried chicken (KFC) and dumplings, and a line of tacos and burritos that uses locally sourced ingredients and naturally raised meat. Classic bibimbap served with *ban chan* (side dishes) is also available. As you listen to soft reggae, sip a soju cocktail, and tuck into a plate of savory tacos, you'll wish this joint were on the corner of your own street.

KOREAN TACOS

At Little Dokebi, diners can choose from tacos filled with short ribs, pork shoulder, chicken, tofu, or wild mushrooms. Simmering the taco fillings with spicy, zesty barbecue sauce just before serving them is the key to their flavor.

MAKES 6 TACOS

Dokebi Barbecue Sauce:

¼ cup chopped garlic

½ onion, coarsely chopped

1 fresh or canned pineapple ring, chopped

½ kiwi, peeled and chopped

½ Asian pear, peeled, halved, and cored

½ cup soy sauce

1 cup water

One 1-inch piece fresh ginger, peeled and smashed

½ lemon, cut in half

½ orange, cut crosswise

1 teaspoon granulated sugar, or more to taste

¼ cup sesame oil

2 teaspoons finely ground dried red chili pepper (optional)

Scallion Topping:

1 tablespoon soy sauce

1 teaspoon sesame oil

Pinch of granulated sugar

1 bunch scallions, trimmed and finely chopped

1 cup shredded red-leaf lettuce or red cabbage

Taco Fillings:

2 tablespoons vegetable oil

1½ pounds short rib meat, cut into long rectangles, or

1½ pounds boneless pork shoulder, cut into small strips, or

1½ pounds skinless; boneless chicken breasts, cut into small strips, or

1½ pounds firm tofu, drained and cut into small strips, or

1½ pounds mixed cremini, shiitake, maitake, and oyster mushrooms, chopped

Twelve 6-inch corn tortillas

1 bunch radishes, trimmed and thinly sliced, for serving

To make the barbecue sauce: Put the garlic, onion, pineapple, kiwi, and pear in a food processor and pulse until finely chopped.

Transfer the pineapple mixture to a large saucepan, add the soy sauce and water, and bring to a boil. Add the ginger, lemon, orange, and sugar and simmer until the sauce has reduced by about one quarter, about 30 minutes. Remove from the heat and let cool.

Strain the sauce into a bowl; discard the solids. Add the sesame oil and chili pepper, if using, and stir well to combine. Taste and adjust the seasonings. The sauce will keep, covered, in the refrigerator for up to a month. Bring to room temperature and shake well before using.

To make the scallion topping: Whisk the soy sauce, sesame oil, and sugar together in a small bowl. Put the scallions and lettuce in a medium bowl, add the soy sauce mixture, and toss together. Set aside.

To make each of the taco fillings: Heat the vegetable oil in a large skillet over medium-high heat until shimmering. Add the meat, chicken, tofu, or mushrooms and sauté until cooked and lightly browned. Ladle about ½ cup of the barbecue sauce over the filling and stir until well coated, adding more if needed.

For each taco, stack 2 corn tortillas in a dry skillet and heat them until they just begin to brown. Turn and cook on the other side until just browned. Spoon some of the desired fillings onto the warm tortillas. Top with some scallion topping and radishes, and serve.

KIM CHI BLOODY MARY

SERVES 6

Bloody Mary Mix:

One 46-ounce bottle tomato
or vegetable juice

2 tablespoons fresh lemon juice

2 tablespoons fresh lime juice

2 tablespoons prepared horseradish

1 tablespoon Worcestershire sauce

Dash of Tabasco sauce

1 tablespoon green olive brine

2 tablespoons kimchi juice

Freshly ground black pepper

12 ounces vodka

½ cup kimchi

Tabasco sauce (optional)

Freshly ground black pepper
(optional)

Green olives, lemon and lime wedges,
and celery sticks, for garnish

The Bloody Mary may be best known as a hangover remedy to drink at brunch. Little Dokebi serves a fantastic version that is spiced with liquid from pungent Korean kimchi, and it's certainly not for brunch only.

To prepare the Bloody Mary mix: Combine the tomato, lemon and lime juices, horseradish, Worcestershire and Tabasco sauces, olive brine, kimchi juice, and pepper to taste in a jar or other large container with a tight-fitting lid. Cover tightly and shake vigorously. Chill in the refrigerator. (The mix can be made up to 2 days ahead.)

Fill six tall glasses with ice cubes. Add 2 ounces vodka to each one, top off with Bloody Mary mix, and stir. Add a generous spoonful of kimchi to each glass and stir again. For extra spiciness, add more Tabasco sauce and pepper. Garnish each drink with olives, lemon and lime wedges, and a celery stick.

PINEAPPLE-INFUSED SOJU COCKTAIL

SERVES 6 TO 8

One 750-ml bottle soju

2 cups 1-inch pieces fresh
   pineapple (about 16 chunks)

Soju is a sake-like rice liquor that has a smooth, clean taste that goes very well with Korean food. At Little Dokebi, it is infused with fresh pineapple and served chilled in small glasses. It makes a very refreshing, light cocktail.

Pour the soju into a clean container with a lid. Add the pineapple pieces, cover, and chill in the refrigerator for at least 8 hours. (The infused soju will keep, covered, in the refrigerator for up to 2 days.)

Pour the soju into small glasses, garnish with the pineapple pieces, and serve.

ACHILLES HEEL

180 WEST STREET

Compared to Brooklyn restaurateur Andrew Tarlow's other high-profile spots, Reynard, Diner, and Marlow & Sons, Achilles Heel is positively laid-back. And that's fine with the locals who come to this café-bar for coffee in the morning and for drinks in the evening. Situated on a quiet corner of the Greenpoint waterfront, it was once a grocery and bar that served dock-workers in the late nineteenth century. Certain original details from that era, like the bar mantel, hardwood floors, and mirrors, are part of this comfortable space. Achilles Heel serves great cocktails and well-chosen beers and wines along with a terrific selection of bar bites: oysters, Portugese sardines, pickled eggs, country pâté, and more.

PICKLED EGGS

Hard-boiled eggs pickled in a vinegar brine with fresh beets make a wonderful cocktail appetizer. These bright-pink beauties are also great to serve at picnics and parties.

MAKES 2 DOZEN PICKLED EGGS

2 dozen large eggs

3 cups distilled white vinegar

1 cup boiling water

1/4 cup kosher salt

1/4 cup granulated sugar

1 1/2 teaspoons black peppercorns

1 1/2 teaspoons allspice berries

1 1/2 teaspoons coriander seeds

1 1/2 teaspoons juniper berries

1 star anise

1 bay leaf

1 small cinnamon stick

1/2 cup peeled and thinly sliced red beets

Extra-virgin olive oil, for serving

Sea salt and freshly ground black pepper

Fill a large stockpot with water and bring to a rolling boil. Carefully drop the eggs into the pot and cook for 9 minutes. Drain and transfer the eggs to a large bowl filled with ice.

When they are cool enough to handle, peel the eggs. Set aside.

Put the vinegar, boiling water, kosher salt, sugar, peppercorns, allspice, coriander, juniper berries, star anise, bay leaf, cinnamon stick, and beets in a large clean jar with a lid and stir well to dissolve the salt and sugar. Add the eggs, cover, and refrigerate for 1 week before using.

To serve, cut the eggs lengthwise in half, drizzle with olive oil, and sprinkle with sea salt and pepper.

COUNTRY PÂTÉ

This recipe comes from Matthew Dale, the head butcher at Marlow & Daughters, and it's a stunner. Don't be put off by the long ingredient list and the prep time involved. Making your own highly seasoned, rich, and hearty pâté is immensely satisfying, and the extra labor will pay off in flavor in the end. Accompanied by crusty bread, strong mustard, and a few pickles, this country pâté is great to serve to a crowd.

MAKES TWO 3-POUND PÂTÉS
SPECIAL EQUIPMENT: MEAT GRINDER; TWO 11 BY 3-INCH TERRINE MOLDS

2 tablespoons unsalted butter

1 shallot, finely sliced

2 garlic cloves, thinly sliced

Pinch of kosher salt

¼ cup cognac or other brandy

2 teaspoons black peppercorns

1 teaspoon white peppercorns

½ teaspoon allspice berries

1 whole clove

1 bay leaf

1 teaspoon cayenne pepper

1 teaspoon freshly grated nutmeg

1 teaspoon mustard seeds

1 teaspoon pink salt (optional)

4 pounds boneless lean pork, trimmed of sinew and cut into 2-inch cubes

1¾ pounds skinless pork belly or fatback, cut into 2-inch cubes

2 teaspoons chopped fresh thyme

2 teaspoons chopped fresh flat-leaf parsley

1 cup dry white wine

About 20 thin slices smoked bacon, for lining the terrines

At least 2 days before serving, melt the butter in a medium skillet over medium-high heat. Once the butter stops foaming, add the shallots, garlic, and 1½ teaspoons salt, tossing to combine. Cook for 5 to 10 minutes, until the shallots and garlic start to brown and caramelize. Deglaze the pan with the cognac, stirring and scraping up the browned bits on the bottom of the pan. Reduce the heat and cook until the mixture is golden brown, 5 to 10 minutes. Transfer to a plate and let cool to room temperature.

Heat a small skillet over medium heat. Add the peppercorns, allspice berries, clove, and bay leaf and toast until fragrant, about 2 minutes. Transfer to a spice grinder and grind into a fine powder. Transfer to a small bowl, add the cayenne pepper, nutmeg, mustard seeds, and pink salt, if using, and stir together.

Put the pork and pork belly cubes in a large bowl. Add the shallot and spice mixtures, the thyme, and the parsley and mix thoroughly. Cover and refrigerate overnight.

The next day, chill the meat grinder parts for 30 minutes in the freezer.

Pass the meat mixture (referred to in the butcher world as a *farce*) through the medium-size grinding plate into a chilled bowl. Add the wine and mix thoroughly with your hands until the *farce* is sticky and has a fair amount of tack to it. A good test is to make a small patty, press it against your palm, and turn your hand over. If the patty sticks, it is mixed appropriately.

Prepare the terrine molds by lining them with the bacon, which will act as the wrapping of the pâté: Arrange the slices in evenly spaced rows, edge to edge, so that they cover the bottom of the molds and hang over the edges by a few inches on all sides.

Pack the *farce* forcefully into the molds, pressing it down and shaking and banging the molds on the counter as you go to ensure that there are no air bubbles. Once the meat is in place, fold the ends of the bacon over, making sure the surface is covered. Cover each pâté with a double layer of aluminum foil, making sure it is tight around the edges. Put the prepared pâtés in the refrigerator for 1 hour.

Preheat the oven to 250°F.

Put the terrines in a large baking pan. Fill the pan with enough hot water to reach halfway up the sides of the molds. Cover the whole pan with foil and put it in the oven. Bake for 1½ to 2 hours, or until the internal temperature of each pâté reads 145°F in the center.

Remove the pâtés from the water bath. Put a piece of cardboard cut to the size of the pâté on top of each. Weight the pâtés with heavy cans or weights and let them cool to room temperature, then still weighted, refrigerate overnight.

To serve, unmold the pâtés and trim the sides of any fat or solidified juices that have accumulated. Cut into slices with a sharp knife.

LUCKY DOG

SERVES 1

Kosher salt

1 small lemon, lime,
   or grapefruit wedge

1½ ounces Luksusowa vodka

¾ ounce Campari

¾ ounce fresh grapefruit juice

¼ ounce Simple Syrup (page 16)

Pour some salt onto a small shallow plate. Rub the rim of a highball glass with the lemon wedge and dip the glass into the plate of salt to coat the rim. Fill the glass with ice.

Fill a cocktail shaker with ice. Add the vodka, Campari, grapefruit juice, and simple syrup and shake vigorously. Strain into the prepared glass and serve.

FERNET OLD-FASHIONED

SERVES 1

2 ounces Rittenhouse rye

$\frac{1}{2}$ ounce Fernet Branca bitters

$\frac{1}{2}$ ounce Honey Simple Syrup (see below)

1 orange twist, for garnish

Put the rye, bitters, and simple syrup in a mixing glass. Add ice to fill and stir well. Strain into a rocks glass filled with ice, garnish with the orange twist, and serve.

To make the Honey Simple Syrup: Combine equal parts honey and hot water and stir well until the honey has dissolved. Let cool. The syrup will keep, covered, in the refrigerator for up to a week.

BONE DIAMOND

SERVES 1

$\frac{3}{4}$ ounce Unión mezcal

$\frac{3}{4}$ ounce dry gin

$\frac{3}{4}$ ounce Meletti amaro

$\frac{3}{4}$ ounce fresh orange juice

$\frac{1}{4}$ ounce fresh lemon juice

Fill a cocktail shaker with ice. Add the mezcal, gin, amaro, and orange and lemon juices and shake vigorously. Strain into a rocks glass and serve.

BROOKLYN BEER BARS AND GASTROPUBS

by Ethan Fixell

One need not be a New Yorker to know that Brooklyn brews are some of the best beers in the country. Word of top-notch breweries such as Other Half Brewing Co., Threes Brewing, and KelSo Beer has begun to reach beer fans around the world. Furthermore, established outfits such as Sixpoint Brewery and Brooklyn Brewery (now one of the largest craft brewers in the United States) have been distributing their precious products far beyond the borders of New York State for years.

But the one Brooklyn beer experience unattainable outside New York is to be had reveling in one of its inimitable watering holes. In addition to making great beer, Brooklyn also lays claim to corralling the best beer from all over the world within the boundaries of a single borough. It is home to a number of unique bars and gastropubs offering stellar suds and the perfect eats to go with them.

Of course, New York City is a monstrous territory, and Brooklyn is its most populated borough; unearthing the many treasures of the entire area could fill several books. The following can't-miss spots are the highlights of the two northernmost areas of Brooklyn, Williamsburg and Greenpoint, which also happen to be closest to Manhattan and most soaked with beer.

BARCADE, 388 Union Avenue, Brooklyn, NY 11211

Offering top-notch craft beer and more than fifty retro arcade video games, Barcade is sheer heaven for any nostalgic, thirsty adult. The original Williamsburg location lacks a kitchen, but the bar sells snacks such as pretzels, potato chips, beer nuts, and beef jerky to sop up the tasty suds. The emphasis is always on "local," and most of the two dozen taps pour beer from the community or nearby cities and states. There's nothing like the lofty warehouse feel of the original establishment, but Barcade's owners have since opened two locations in Manhattan that serve excellent food whipped up by Chef Lee Knoeppel, as well as branches in Jersey City and Philadelphia.

MUGS ALEHOUSE, 125 Bedford Avenue, Brooklyn, NY 11211

If Barcade's vast selection isn't enough for you, Mugs Alehouse features more than thirty-five rotating taps offering beer from all over the world, including a monthly special that goes for $2.00 per pint at all hours. The vibe of this old school–style tavern, where blue-collar meets hipster chic, is laid-back and unpretentious. But the eats are better than the average pub grub: Visitors should try the fish and chips (featuring Atlantic cod with a Brooklyn Lager batter), the lamb and beef shepherd's pie, and "The Williamsburger"—garnished with roasted shiitakes, caramelized onions, cheddar, and Brooklyn Lager BBQ sauce.

SPUYTEN DUYVIL, 359 Metropolitan Avene, Brooklyn, NY 11211

On the hunt for rare beer? Look no farther than Spuyten Duyvil, which boasts a bottle list featuring over a hundred of some of the most obscure and hard-to-come-by brews on earth. Fans of Belgian and German sour and imperial styles will find bliss in this aged-beer haven. The food menu is limited, but what more does one need than plates of gourmet cheese, meat, and Brooklyn-made pickles to accompany a goblet of the heavenly stuff? You'll likely spend a premium at this rare beer mecca, but any self-professed beer nerd needs to make the pilgrimage at least once (and many more times, if he or she can afford it).

BROUWERIJ LANE, 78 Greenpoint Avenue, Brooklyn, NY 11222

For the true collector, a stop at Brouwerij Lane (pronounced "brow-er-eye," Dutch for—you guessed it—brewery) is essential. Here one can build a beer collection from an impeccably curated list of more than 150 bottles. Best of all, this Greenpoint shop is also equipped with nineteen taps, doubling as a small saloon for parched passersby or those who can't wait to drink a newfound prize at home. You won't find food here, but the ambiance alone—think "old-timey pickle shop"—makes this joint like no other bar in New York, and certainly worth a visit.

DIRCK THE NORSEMAN, 7 North 15th Street, Brooklyn, NY 11222

Brouwerij Lane founder Ed Raven named his second venture after the first European settler of Greenpoint. Though Dirck was Scandinavian, his namesake brewpub pays homage to the many European immigrants (mostly Polish) now inhabiting the area, with traditional dishes such as braised pig's knuckle, potato pierogies, and matzoh ball soup. But as the home to Greenpoint Beer & Ale Company (the only craft brewery in the neighborhood), Dirck's true draw is the beer, which doesn't get any fresher. Of course, Eurocentric purists may prefer to wrap their mitts around a liter of legit German Kölsch, Pilsner, or Weizenbock, all of which are available alternatives to local brew.

TØRST, 615 Manhattan Avene, Brooklyn, NY 11222

Jeppe Jarnit-Bjergsø of Evil Twin Brewing met Noma head pastry chef Daniel Burns when Bjergsø was helping the two-Michelin-star restaurant in Copenhagen with its beer menu. The two have since created one of the most beautiful taprooms in the world, serving fantastic beer along with a killer bar menu. At Tørst (Danish for "thirst," and pronounced similarly), one can sip some of Evil Twin's more uncommon offerings while nibbling on Welsh rarebit, smoked trout, or duck confit sandwiches. The food is crafted by Burns, who earned a Michelin star of his own at Luksus, Tørst's adjoining restaurant, which offers an out-of-this-world fifteen-course tasting menu with beer pairings.

BUSHWICK

Bushwick, a rapidly transforming neighborhood, is home to a diverse population. It boasts a thriving art scene, with more than fifty galleries and alternative art spaces in the heart of its industrial landscape. It is also a flourishing restaurant and bar spot that draws food-lovers from all over the city.

DEAR BUSHWICK

41 WILSON AVENUE

You wouldn't expect to find a warm English country kitchen and bar on a rather nondescript street in an industrial area of Bushwick. But Dear Bushwick is exactly that. In 2012, Julian Mohamed and Darren Grenia opened this charming outpost that is outfitted with wooden tables, weathered shutters, and pressed tin ceilings, and decorated with British flea market finds throughout. Grenia has created a formidable cocktail menu that features a number of original gin- and whiskey-based libations. Chef Jessica Wilson, who has cooked at Goat Town, A Voce, and Prune restaurants, creates utterly delicious rustic dishes using locally sourced meat, fish, and produce. Think fried potato peels dusted with salt and vinegar, juicy oysters under a crumble of warm bread crumbs, and seared pork belly with cracklings.

ROASTED OYSTERS

This is a wonderful way to serve oysters without the shucking: They pop open after about 10 minutes of roasting in the oven. Chef Wilson serves them drizzled with fresh orange juice, olive oil, and herbs, but she suggests that they could also be served with almost any type of oyster sauce or condiment, such as an aioli, cocktail sauce, or chutney of your choice.

SERVES 6

2 dozen medium oysters, scrubbed

6 thick slices country bread

Unsalted butter or olive oil, for brushing

Juice of ½ orange

Extra-virgin olive oil, for drizzling

Sea salt and freshly ground black pepper

1 cup chopped mixed fresh herbs, such as flat-leaf parsley, basil, cilantro, and mint

Preheat the oven to 375°F.

Arrange the oysters, rounded side down, on a baking sheet. Roast until the oysters start to pop open, about 10 minutes. Meanwhile, grill or toast the bread and brush with butter. Remove the oysters from the oven and, with an oyster knife or other small sharp knife, carefully remove the top shells from each one and detach the oysters from the bottom shells, keeping the liquid in the shells.

Arrange the oysters on a platter or individual plates. Drizzle them with the orange juice and olive oil, sprinkle with sea salt and pepper to taste, and garnish with the herbs. Serve with the toast.

BRAISED PORK BELLY

WITH WHIPPED CARROTS & STEWED SEASONAL FRUIT

Pork belly, a fatty boneless cut from the belly of a pig, was once considered to be scrap meat and relegated to soups and stews by frugal cooks. Today it has become a favorite of chefs because of its rich, mellow flavor and meltingly tender texture. Pork belly should be braised, stewed, or slow-roasted ahead of time and refrigerated overnight before searing, so it's a perfect make-ahead dinner party entrée.

SERVES 6

Rub:

¼ cup black peppercorns

3 garlic cloves, minced

3 bay leaves, crushed

4 fresh thyme sprigs, chopped

1 cup packed brown sugar
  or granulated sugar

1 cup kosher salt

4 pounds pork belly, skin removed

Whipped Carrots (recipe follows)

Stewed Seasonal Fruit (recipe follows)

Extra-virgin olive oil, for serving

Freshly ground black pepper

Chopped mixed fresh herbs,
  such as flat-leaf parsley, dill, and mint,
  for garnish (optional)

To make the rub: The day before serving, put the peppercorns, garlic, bay leaves, thyme, sugar, and salt in a large bowl and mix together.

Rub the mixture evenly over all sides of the pork belly. Transfer to a container with a lid, cover tightly, and refrigerate overnight.

Preheat the oven to 400°F.

Line a baking sheet with parchment paper and arrange the pork belly on it. Bake for 30 minutes. Reduce the heat to 350°F and bake for 1 hour more. Reduce the heat to 250°F and bake for an additional hour. Remove from the oven and let the pork belly rest for 30 minutes.

Wrap the pork belly tightly in plastic wrap and let it chill completely in the refrigerator. (The braised pork belly can be slow-roasted ahead of time. It will keep, covered, in the refrigerator for up to a week.)

Cut the pork belly into 6 equal slabs. Sear in a large cast-iron or nonstick pan until browned on all four sides, about 3 minutes per side.

To serve, spoon the whipped carrots onto individual plates or a large platter. Arrange the pork belly slabs over them and top with the stewed fruit. Drizzle with olive oil, sprinkle with pepper, and garnish with fresh herbs, if desired.

WHIPPED CARROTS

4 cups peeled and chopped carrots

1 teaspoon kosher salt

$\frac{1}{2}$ cup neutral oil, such as grapeseed, canola, or olive oil

Put the carrots and salt in medium saucepan, add water to cover, and bring to a boil. Reduce the heat to medium and cook until fork-tender, 10 to 15 minutes. Drain the carrots and reserve $\frac{1}{2}$ cup of cooking water. Transfer the carrots to a food processor or blender. Add a bit of the reserved water and the oil and blend until smooth, adding more water if needed. The carrots can be served warm or chilled. If serving warm, reheat them in a small pan over low heat.

STEWED SEASONAL FRUIT

1 pint seasonal or dried fruit,
  such as orange segments,
  blackberries, blueberries, or raisins
1 cup granulated sugar
¼ cup champagne vinegar

2 bay leaves
3 fresh thyme sprigs
Freshly ground black pepper
2 cups water

Put the fruit, sugar, vinegar, bay leaves, thyme, pepper to taste, and water in a medium saucepan and bring to a low boil. Reduce the heat and let simmer for 10 minutes. Serve warm.

St. George

SERVES 1

1 teaspoon Cucumber Tincture
  (recipe follows)

¼ ounce Simple Syrup (page 16)

¼ ounce St-Germain
  elderflower liqueur

2 ounces St. George Botanivore gin

1 lime peel, for garnish

Cucumber Tincture:
MAKES ABOUT 4 CUPS

1 large cucumber, peeled
  and chopped

One 750-ml bottle Everclear

Fill a mixing glass with ice. Add the tincture, simple syrup, liqueur, and gin, stir for 20 seconds, and strain into an ice-filled old-fashioned glass. Express the lime peel over the drink, run it around the rim of the glass, and serve.

To make the Cucumber Tincture: Put the chopped cucumber in a 1-quart jar with a lid. Pour in the Everclear, cover, and let the mixture sit for 2 hours in the refrigerator.

Strain the mixture through a funnel lined with two coffee filters into another container. Press hard on the solids to get all the liquid out. Pour it back into the jar. It will keep, covered, in the refrigerator indefinitely.

SMOKING JACKET

SERVES 1

4 drops Bittermens Xocolati
    Mole bitters

¼ ounce Chili Stout Reduction
    (recipe follows)

½ ounce bottled or
    fresh ginger syrup (see below)

¾ ounce fresh lime juice

2 ounces El Peletón
    de la Muerte mezcal

Chili Stout Reduction:

MAKES ABOUT 1½ CUPS

One 12-ounce can Lion Stout
    or other dark thick stout

3 cups Sugar In The Raw

1 teaspoon chili powder

Fill a cocktail shaker with ice. Add the bitters, stout reduction, ginger syrup, lime juice, and mezcal and shake vigorously for 10 to 15 seconds. Strain into a chilled cocktail glass and serve.

To make the Chili Stout Reduction: Slowly pour the stout into a saucepan. Add the sugar and cook over low heat, stirring frequently to dissolve the sugar; make sure that the mixture does not boil. Add the chili powder and simmer for 5 minutes. Remove from the heat and let cool to room temperature. The reduction will keep, covered, in the refrigerator for up to 3 weeks.

To make fresh ginger syrup: Blend ½ cup peeled and chopped fresh ginger and 1 cup superfine sugar in a Vitamix or other high-powered blender until the sugar has dissolved.

NO. 7

7 GREENE AVENUE

Located at the busy corner of Fulton Street and Greene Avenue, American bistro No. 7 is a warm, welcoming spot that has the feel of an old-fashioned train station lounge. Chef Tyler Kord's dishes soar above and beyond the Brooklyn comfort food zone. A graduate of The French Culinary Institute and a Jean-Georges Vongerichten restaurant alum, Kord opened No. 7 in 2008. There he serves imaginative and delicious riffs on traditional dishes such as grilled Caesar salad, steamed mussels, and fried broccoli tacos. And the cocktails at No. 7—Deep Mountain Sazerac, Laura Palmer, Happy/Sad Girl—are as haunting and luscious as their names.

FORT GREENE

Fort Greene is a wonderfully diverse neighborhood in northwest Brooklyn. Steeped in history, with tree-lined streets and beautiful brownstones, the area is home to the Brooklyn Academy of Music, Pratt Institute, Fort Greene Park, and the can't-miss Brooklyn Flea, the city's foremost vintage bazaar.

STEAMED BOUCHOT MUSSELS
WITH HOMEMADE CHORIZO

The chorizo at No. 7 is made in-house. Chef Kord says, "This recipe makes way too much for the mussels, but it's delicious and you can use it for lots of other things, like adding it to soups, stews, and eggs." It also freezes beautifully. Look for big, meaty Bouchot mussels from Maine, but any type of mussel will do in this dish.

SERVES 6 TO 8

Chorizo:

3½ ounces (half a can) chipotles in adobo sauce

3 garlic cloves

1½ tablespoons kosher salt

3 tablespoons distilled white vinegar

2 tablespoons St-Germain elderflower liqueur

1 star anise

5 whole cloves

½ cinnamon stick

3 pounds ground pork

1 tablespoon Korean red chili powder

½ teaspoon sesame oil

1 cup canned tomatoes in tomato puree

1 cup dry white wine

3 pounds mussels, preferably Bouchot, scrubbed and debearded

2 cups thinly sliced napa cabbage

1 teaspoon kosher salt

1 tablespoon unsalted butter

1 cup fresh Thai basil leaves

Preheat the oven to 400°F.

To make the chorizo: Put the chipotles, garlic, salt, vinegar, liqueur, star anise, cloves, and cinnamon in a blender and blend until smooth. Transfer to a large bowl. Add the ground pork, chili powder, and sesame oil and mix thoroughly.

Put the pork mixture on a large baking sheet and spread it evenly. Bake until firm to the touch and cooked through, about 10 minutes. Remove from the oven.

When it is cool enough to handle, crumble the chorizo. Reserve 2 cups for this dish and refrigerate the rest for another use.

Put the tomatoes and wine in a blender and blend until smooth.

Put the mussels, cabbage, salt, the 2 cups chorizo, and the tomato-and-wine mixture in a large pot, bring to a boil over high heat, cover, and cook just until the mussels have opened, about 3 to 6 minutes. Discard any unopened mussels. Add the butter and basil leaves and mix thoroughly.

Spoon the mussels with their liquid into shallow bowls and serve.

GRILLED ROMAINE CAESAR SALAD
WITH FRIED SOFT-BOILED EGG

This is the Caesar salad of your dreams. It is packed with bold flavors and has lots of tasty crunch in every bite. You should always make a few extra eggs to make sure that you have enough with just the right degree of runniness when they're split open over the salads.

SERVES 6

Caesar Dressing:

2 garlic cloves

3 tablespoons Dijon mustard

1 tablespoon gochujang paste (see Note)

2 tablespoons white wine vinegar

2 tablespoons fresh lemon juice

1 teaspoon kosher salt

1 cup extra-virgin olive oil

Fried Soft-Boiled Eggs:

8 large eggs

3 large egg whites

$\frac{1}{2}$ cup cornstarch

1 cup panko bread crumbs

Vegetable oil for deep-frying

Extra-virgin olive oil

3 heads romaine lettuce, large outer leaves removed, split in half lengthwise

Kosher salt

$\frac{1}{2}$ cup freshly grated Parmesan cheese

12 anchovy fillets

$\frac{1}{2}$ small red onion, sliced into very thin rounds

Freshly ground black pepper

To make the dressing: Put the garlic, mustard, gochujang paste, vinegar, lemon juice, and salt in a blender and blend until smooth. Slowly drizzle in the olive oil, blending again until smooth.

To make the eggs: Fill a large stockpot halfway with water and bring to a boil over high heat. Gently lower the eggs into the water and boil them for exactly 7 minutes. With a slotted spoon, transfer the eggs to a bowl filled with ice water. When cool enough to handle, drain and peel the eggs.

Combine the raw egg whites and cornstarch in a small bowl and whisk until the cornstarch is fully dissolved and the mixture is smooth. Spread the panko out on a plate or in a shallow bowl. Dip an egg in the egg white mixture, let the excess drain off, and gently toss it in the panko, then put it on a plate. Repeat the process with the rest of the eggs.

Pour 3 inches of oil into a large heavy-bottomed pot, and heat over medium-high heat to 400°F. Add the eggs and fry, turning occasionally, until golden brown, 2 to 3 minutes. Remove from the oil and drain on paper towels.

Heat an outdoor grill or a grill pan. Drizzle olive oil over the lettuce halves and season lightly with salt. Grill cut side down until the lettuce just begins to char, about 2 minutes. Remove from the heat.

To serve, arrange the lettuce halves on six plates. Drizzle each one with a tablespoon of the dressing and sprinkle with some of the Parmesan. Slice one egg in half over one of the salads, trying not to lose too much yolk, and arrange on the salad. Repeat with the remaining eggs. Top each salad with 2 anchovy fillets, some sliced red onion, and a sprinkling of pepper.

Note: Gochujang is a Korean hot pepper paste. It is available at Asian markets and online.

LAURA PALMER

SERVES 1

¾ ounce Italian Brandy

¾ ounce Orgeat (recipe follows)

Champagne

Orgeat:

4 cups unsweetened almond milk

4 cups granulated sugar

2 ounces amaretto

2 ounces almond extract

½ ounce rose water

Fill a cocktail shaker with ice. Add the brandy and Orgeat and shake vigorously. Strain into a chilled coupe, top off with Champagne, and serve.

To make the Orgeat: Put the almond milk, sugar, amaretto, almond extract, and rose water in a large saucepan and cook over low heat, stirring occasionally, until the sugar has dissolved. Transfer to a container and refrigerate, uncovered, until ready to use. It will keep, covered, for up to 2 weeks.

ALWAYS IN SEASON

SERVES 1

2 tablespoons chopped canned peaches

¾ ounce white rum

¾ ounce Ron Diplomático Reserva
    Exclusiva rum

¾ ounce Aperol

¼ ounce fresh lemon juice

Club soda

Muddle the peaches in a cocktail shaker. Add
the rums, Aperol, and lemon juice and shake
vigorously. Pour into an old-fashioned glass,
top off with a splash of club soda, and serve.

DEEP MOUNTAIN SAZERAC

SERVES 1

2½ ounces Old Overholt rye

½ ounces Deep Mountain Vermont
    maple syrup, preferably Grade B

2 dashes Peychaud's bitters

2 dashes Angostura bitters

Green Chartreuse,
    for rinsing the glass

Fill an old-fashioned glass with ice water to chill it.
Fill a cocktail shaker with ice. Add the rye, maple
syrup, and bitters and shake vigorously. Pour out
the ice water and rinse the glass with the Chartreuse.
Strain the cocktail into the glass and serve.

STONEHOME WINE BAR

87 LAFAYETTE AVENUE

Stonehome Wine Bar has been a welcome outpost in the Fort Greene neighborhood since 2003. Sommelier and owner Bill Stenehjehm and his wife, Rose Hermann, preside over this elegant wine bar that has received *Wine Spectator*'s Award of Excellence annually since 2008. Chef John Gibson serves small plates and bar snacks such as tasty house-marinated olives, pâtés, salads, and well-sourced cheese and charcuterie plates that pair beautifully with the bar's world-class wines, spirits, and beer. More substantial pasta, fish, and game dishes are also on the menu. Stonehome is a convenient, lovely spot for theater- and opera-goers, who frequently stop in for a drink and a bite before or after a show at the nearby Brooklyn Academy of Music.

ROASTED BEET SALAD

WITH GRAPEFRUIT, SHAVED FENNEL
& CANDIED SUNFLOWER SEEDS

Chef Gibson prepares generous amounts of the candied sunflower seeds and citrus vinaigrette used in this salad. The sunflower seeds are great for snacking, and they can also be added to yogurt. The vinaigrette keeps in the refrigerator for up to 4 days, and it is wonderful drizzled over greens, vegetables, or grains. Although you can use any type of watercress in this recipe, do look for Upland peppercress, which has a distinct peppery flavor.

SERVES 4

Candied Sunflower Seeds:

2 cups raw sunflower seeds

1 tablespoon unsalted butter, melted

2 tablespoons granulated sugar

1 tablespoon chopped fresh thyme

1 large egg white, beaten

1 tablespoon kosher salt

Freshly ground black pepper

6 to 8 small beets in assorted colors

Citrus Vinaigrette:

1 large red grapefruit

3 tablespoons fresh orange juice

1 small shallot, minced

1 teaspoon chopped fresh thyme

1 tablespoon honey

1 tablespoon Dijon mustard

½ cup canola or other neutral oil

¼ cup extra-virgin olive oil

Kosher salt and freshly ground black pepper

1 small shallot, finely minced

1 tablespoon finely minced fresh mint

Kosher salt and freshly ground black pepper

1 small fennel bulb, trimmed and thinly shaved on a mandoline

2 cups peppercress or watercress

To make the sunflower seeds: Preheat the oven to 300°F.

Put the sunflower seeds, butter, sugar, thyme, egg white, salt, and pepper to taste in a medium bowl and toss together until the seeds are evenly coated. Spread the seeds out on a nonstick baking sheet and bake for 6 minutes. Stir and bake until toasted, 4 to 6 minutes longer. Remove from the oven and let cool. Increase the oven temperature to 350°F.

Once the sunflower seeds are cool, break up any large clumps. Store in a tightly covered container for up to 1 week.

Put the beets in a small roasting pan and roast until fork-tender, 50 to 60 minutes. Remove and let cool.

Peel the beets and cut them into small pieces, then transfer to a large salad bowl.

To make the citrus vinaigrette: Cut the grapefruit into segments, catching its juice in a bowl as you work; reserve the segments and juice separately.

Put the grapefruit and orange juices in a small saucepan and cook over medium heat until reduced to 3 tablespoons. Transfer to a blender; add the shallot, thyme, honey, and mustard and blend until smooth. With the blender running, slowly drizzle in the canola oil and then the olive oil, blending until smooth. Add salt and pepper to taste.

Add the shallot and mint to the beets and toss together. Add enough vinaigrette to coat, along with salt and pepper to taste, and toss again. Arrange the beets on four chilled salad plates. Put the fennel in the salad bowl, add a bit more vinaigrette and salt and pepper to taste, and toss together. Spoon the fennel over the beets.

Arrange the grapefruit segments over the fennel, sprinkle with the sunflower seeds, top with the cress, and serve.

MARINATED OLIVES

The marinated olives at Stonehome Wine Bar pair beautifully with their wines and charcuterie and cheese plates. Although they're delicious served at room temperature, these really shine when they're warmed up. Be sure to have lots of crusty bread on hand to dip in the marinade.

MAKES ABOUT 1 QUART

4 cups mixed olives in brine

2 cups extra-virgin olive oil

10 garlic cloves

Zest of 2 lemons

1 tablespoon fennel seeds

1 teaspoon red pepper flakes

2 tablespoons chopped fresh rosemary

Drain the olives and reserve about 1 cup of the brine. Transfer the olives to a large bowl or container.

Heat the olive oil in a small saucepan over medium-low heat. Add the garlic and cook until tender and lightly browned. Remove from the heat, add the lemon zest, fennel seeds, red pepper flakes, and rosemary, and let steep for 20 minutes.

Pour the olive oil mixture and the reserved brine over the olives and gently stir. Cover and refrigerate for a day before serving.

Bring the olives to room temperature or heat gently until just warm before serving.

As of press time, we learned that Stonehome Wine Bar has closed.

BAR CHUKO

565 VANDERBILT AVENUE

PROSPECT HEIGHTS
Prospect Heights strikes a perfect balance between the new and the old Brooklyn. It is home to the Brooklyn Museum of Art, Brooklyn Botanical Garden, Brooklyn Public Library, and Barclay's Center, as well as blocks of small well-kept brownstones and new luxury condos. Vanderbilt Avenue, in the heart of the neighborhood, is one of the best streets for eating and drinking in Brooklyn.

An *izakaya* is a Japanese drinking establishment that serves a wide variety of small plates to be shared by everyone at the table. Bar Chuko opened in June 2014 and is the sister restaurant to Chuko Ramen, across the street on Vanderbilt Avenue. This warm and friendly spot serves small plates and yakitori alongside an extensive beverage menu, featuring house-made cocktails, shochu, and Japanese whiskey. The restaurant-savvy owners and chef of Bar Chuko were eager to introduce the concept of izakaya to Brooklyn so locals (and others) could taste and savor a number of different scrumptious dishes to accompany drinks. Judging from the wild popularity of this perpetually packed spot, the izakaya experience has caught on big time.

ASSORTED SKEWERS

The kitchen at Bar Chuko serves a variety of bamboo skewers threaded with bite-size items like chicken, beef, pork belly, shishito peppers, or snow peas and grilled over an izakaya grill. It's best to serve these crispy, juicy, tender skewers just as they come off the grill.

Here are a few tips for grilling:
Soak wooden skewers in cold water overnight so they don't burn on the grill.
When skewering shishito peppers or snow peas, position the skewers in a V-shape to give them more structure when cooking. It also creates a handle and makes it easier to turn the skewers on the grill.

GRILLED CHICKEN SKEWERS

SERVES 6 TO 8

3 pounds skinless, boneless chicken
  breasts and thighs

Sake, for brushing

Kosher salt

Tare (page 104), for brushing

Ginger Scallion Relish (page 105), for garnish

Prepare a grill for medium-high heat.

Cut the chicken into 1 by 1½-inch pieces. Thread 4 pieces on each skewer. Brush with sake and sprinkle with salt.

Grill the chicken, basting with the tare and turning occasionally, until golden brown on all sides, about 8 minutes. Garnish each skewer with some ginger scallion relish and serve.

GRILLED WAGYU SHORTRIB SKEWERS

SERVES 6 TO 8

Marinade:

2 tablespoons chopped garlic

2 tablespoons peeled and chopped
  fresh ginger

½ cup soy sauce

¼ cup mirin

3 tablespoons sesame oil

3 tablespoons granulated sugar

3 pounds Wagyu beef shortribs

To make the marinade: Put the garlic and ginger in a food processor and process to a paste. Add the soy sauce, mirin, sesame oil, and sugar and process until smooth.

Slice the beef against the grain into ¼-inch squares. Put the beef in a large bowl or a Ziploc bag and pour the marinade over it. Cover the bowl with plastic wrap or zip the bag and let the meat marinate in the refrigerator overnight, making sure the meat is submerged.

Prepare a grill for medium-high heat.

Remove the beef from the marinade and discard the marinade. Thread 4 squares of the beef on each skewer, wide side up. Grill the meat until nicely seared on both sides, about 3 minutes a side.

GRILLED SHISHITO PEPPER SKEWERS

SERVES 6 TO 8

30 shishito peppers, stems trimmed

Olive oil cooking spray

Kosher salt

½ cup grated queso fresco

1 tablespoon ichimi pepper

6 lime wedges, for garnish

Prepare a grill for medium-high heat.

Thread 3 to 5 shishito peppers on each skewer. Spray the peppers with cooking spray and sprinkle with salt. Grill the peppers, turning occasionally, until blistered, about 6 to 8 minutes. Sprinkle with the queso fresco and ichimi pepper and serve with the lime wedges.

GRILLED SNOW PEA SKEWERS

SERVES 6 TO 8

8 ounces snow peas

Extra-virgin olive oil

Kosher salt

Sancho pepper

Lemon or lime zest, for garnish

Prepare a grill for medium-high heat.

Thread about 10 snow peas on skewers. Grill the snow peas, turning occasionally, until lightly browned and tender, 7 to 10 minutes. Drizzle with olive oil, sprinkle with salt, sansho pepper, and lemon zest, and serve.

TARE

Tare is a rich, sweet Japanese sauce made from chicken bones, soy sauce, sake, and a healthy dose of garlic. At Bar Chuko, it's brushed onto yakitori (grilled meat skewers) during the cooking process. Tare is also an excellent basting sauce when grilling and broiling meats at home, and it is especially good with chicken wings or thighs.

MAKES ABOUT 2 CUPS

1 whole chicken carcass
   (from a grilled or roasted chicken)
1¼ cups water
1 cup mirin
¾ cup soy sauce
½ cup sake

One 2-inch knob of ginger, cut in half
2 heads garlic, unpeeled, cut crosswise in half
½ bunch scallions, trimmed and chopped
1 teaspoon black peppercorns

Put the chicken carcass, water, mirin, soy sauce, sake, ginger, garlic, scallions, and peppercorns in a large heavy-bottomed pot and bring to a boil. Reduce the heat and simmer until the sauce has reduced and thickened, about 2 hours. Brush the sides of the pot with a wet pastry brush occasionally to prevent the sauce from sticking.

Remove from the heat and let cool to room temperature.

Strain the sauce into a clean container with a lid. The sauce will keep, covered, in the refrigerator for up to a month.

GINGER SCALLION RELISH

This relish is Bar Chuko's garnish for its chicken skewers. The relish is also a tasty condiment to keep on hand to accompany dishes such as grilled fish and vegetables.

MAKES ABOUT 2 1/2 CUPS

8 ounces fresh ginger, peeled
and coarsely chopped

2 garlic cloves

2 bunches scallions, trimmed
and coarsely chopped

2 cups soybean oil

1 teaspoon kosher salt

Freshly ground white pepper

Put the ginger and garlic in a food processor and pulse until finely chopped and well blended. Transfer to a medium heatproof bowl. Put the scallions in the food processor and pulse a few times. Remove and set aside.

Heat the oil to 400°F in a large heavy-bottomed pot. The oil should just be smoking. Pour the hot oil over the ginger-and-garlic mixture. Add the scallions, salt, and a generous amount of white pepper and stir together. Let cool.

Transfer the relish to a clean container with a lid. It will keep, covered, in the refrigerator for up to a month; bring to room temperature before serving.

GROUND PORK RICE BOWL

Rice bowls, composed of simple combinations of rice, meat or fish, vegetables, and eggs, are pure Asian comfort food. Bar Chuko serves a range of delicious rice bowls, and this one, made with ground pork, kimchi, and a fried egg, is especially good.

SERVES 6

5 tablespoons vegetable oil

12 ounces ground pork

1 tablespoon kosher salt, plus more as needed

2 tablespoons gochujang paste

6 large eggs

3 cups cooked short-grain white rice

12 ounces kimchi, drained and chopped

½ cup chopped scallions

Heat 2 tablespoons of the oil in a large sauté pan over medium-high heat. Add the pork and cook, stirring with a spoon constantly, until the pork is broken up. Add the salt and gochujang paste and mix well. Reduce the heat and cook, stirring occasionally, until the pork is cooked through. Remove from the heat.

Meanwhile, heat the remaining 3 tablespoons oil over medium-high heat in a large skillet. Crack the eggs into the pan and cook sunny-side up. Remove from the heat, cover to keep warm, and set aside.

To serve, spoon ½ cup rice into the bottom of each bowl. Spoon up a bit of liquid from the ground pork and drizzle over the rice. Put one-sixth of the ground pork on one side of each bowl. Put one-sixth of the kimchi next to the pork. Sprinkle with some scallions and top each bowl with a fried egg. Sprinkle with salt to taste and serve.

COLD TODDY

SERVES 1

1½ ounces bourbon

1¼ ounces Toddy Syrup
(recipe follows)

½ ounce fresh lemon juice

2 dashes Angostura bitters

1 lemon wheel, studded
with whole cloves,
for garnish

Toddy Syrup:

MAKES 2 CUPS

2 cups water

2 cups granulated sugar

1 cinnamon stick

15 whole cloves

A pinch of ichimi pepper

1 tea bag black tea

Put the bourbon, syrup, lemon juice, and bitters in a cocktail shaker, add ice to fill, cover, and shake well. Strain into a chilled rocks glass. Garnish with the lemon wheel and serve.

To make the Toddy Syrup: Put the water, sugar, cinnamon stick, cloves, and pepper in a saucepan and bring to a boil over medium-high heat, stirring to dissolve the sugar. Remove from the heat, add the tea bag, and let steep until cool, about 30 minutes.

Strain the syrup into a clean container with a lid. The syrup will keep, covered, in the refrigerator for up to 4 weeks.

BELLE HARBOR

SERVES 1

2 ounces Coconut-Infused Rum
  (recipe follows)

½ ounce dry vermouth

½ ounce dry Curaçao

½ ounce Cherry Simple Syrup
  (recipe follows)

2 dashes orange bitters

1 Amarena cherry, for garnish

Coconut Infused Rum:
MAKES ABOUT 1 QUART

5 ounces cold-pressed virgin
  organic coconut oil

One 750-ml bottle Owney's
  Original NYC rum

Cherry Simple Syrup:
MAKES ABOUT 2 CUPS

1 cup granulated sugar

1 cup water

1 cup cherry juice from jarred
  Amarena cherries

This drink is a riff on an El Presidente, a classic pre-Prohibition cocktail.

Put the rum, vermouth, Curaçao, cherry syrup, and bitters in a mixing glass. Add ice to fill and stir until chilled. Strain into a chilled coupe. Garnish with the cherry and serve.

To make the Coconut-Infused Rum: Heat the coconut oil in a small saucepan over medium heat until it becomes liquid. Remove from the heat.

Pour the rum into a 1-quart container and pour in the coconut oil. Seal the container and shake it vigorously about 3 times a day for 3 to 5 days before using.

To make the Cherry Simple Syrup: Combine the sugar and water in a saucepan and bring to a gentle boil over medium-high heat, stirring to dissolve the sugar. Reduce the heat and simmer until the sugar is completely dissolved and the syrup is slightly thickened, about 3 minutes. Remove from the heat and let cool to room temperature.

Add the cherry juice to the syrup and stir well to combine. Transfer to a clean container with a lid, cover, and refrigerate until ready to use. The syrup will keep in the refrigerator for up to a month.

CROWN HEIGHTS

Crown Heights is a diverse, lively neighborhood rich in history, culture, and architecture. It is home to large Caribbean and Hasidic Jewish communities, young families, and students. Excellent restaurants, bars, and shops are springing up all over the area.

TOOKER ALLEY

793 WASHINGTON AVENUE

Tooker Alley's owner Del Pedro, a former bartender at Manhattan's famed Pegu Club, opened his friendly cocktail lounge in Crown Heights in 2012, fashioned after the principles of Chicago's Dil Pickle Club, a local hangout. Tooker Alley is named for the street where the Dil Pickle Club was located from about 1915 to 1930. Its clientele came from all quarters of society, and its motto was "Elevate your mind to a lower level of thinking." With its understated decor and well-curated jazz soundtrack, Tooker Alley is a great neighborhood spot for conversation, eating, and drinking. Chef Evaristo Alvarez serves inventive, delicious bar snacks to accompany a roster of sublime cocktails.

GRILLED-CHEESE PLATE
WITH TOMATO SOUP

Chef Alvarez's unique riff on a cheese plate includes three varieties of cheese—grilled Manchego and Swiss in mini sandwiches and Parmesan grated over tomato soup. The salty, gooey sandwiches are a delicious, crispy bar snack that beg to be dipped in the soup.

SERVES 6

Tomato Soup:

One 32-ounce can whole
   San Marzano tomatoes

1 tablespoon olive oil

¼ Spanish onion, finely chopped

1½ teaspoons dried oregano

1 teaspoon kosher salt

1 teaspoon freshly ground black pepper

2 garlic cloves, minced

Two 5½-ounce cans tomato juice

5 fresh basil leaves, finely chopped

Freshly grated Parmesan cheese,
   for sprinkling

Sandwich #1 (makes 6 small sandwiches):

¼ cup mayonnaise

12 slices sourdough bread,
   cut into two 3 by 2½-inch squares

About 4½ ounces Manchego cheese,
   cut into six 2 by 2-inch slices

2 tablespoons quince jam

Sandwich #2 (makes 6 small sandwiches):

About 4½ ounces Swiss cheese,
   cut into six 2 by 2-inch slices

6 slices cooked bacon, cut in half

6 slices beefsteak or plum tomatoes, cut in half

12 slices rye bread,
   cut into two 3 by 2½-inch squares

To make the tomato soup: Put the tomatoes in a food processor and pulse until smooth.

Heat the oil in a large skillet over medium heat. Add the onion, oregano, salt, and pepper and cook, stirring, until the onion is softened, about 3 minutes. Add the garlic and cook, stirring, for 30 seconds. Add the pureed tomatoes, tomato juice, and basil and simmer, stirring occasionally, for about 10 minutes to develop the flavors.

To make sandwich #1: Divide the mayonnaise on evenly among the bread and top half of the slices with the cheese. Divide the jam evenly among the remaining slices of bread and gently press the sandwiches together.

To make sandwich #2: Layer the Swiss cheese, bacon, and tomato on half the slices of rye bread. Top with the remaining slices of bread and gently press the sandwiches together. Heat a griddle or a skillet over medium heat. Cook the sandwiches until the bread is golden and the cheese is melted, about 4 minutes per side; cover the griddle or pan to make the cheese melt if necessary.

To serve, arrange one each of both sandwiches on six plates. Pour ¼ cup tomato soup into each of six ramekins and top each portion with a generous pinch of Parmesan cheese.

BIRD ON A WIRE

These delicious chicken tenders served with a pineapple-chili sauce spiked with lime make a great party hors d'oeuvre. The tenders need to brine for a day before being cooked.

SERVES 6

2 quarts water

¼ cup kosher salt

3 pounds chicken tenders

2 tablespoons curry powder

1 tablespoon ground cumin

2 tablespoons minced garlic

2 tablespoons plain yogurt

½ cup olive oil

Pinch of freshly ground black pepper

Pineapple-Chili Sauce:

¼ cup chopped fresh pineapple

Juice of ½ lime

Kosher salt

One 3½-ounce jar Thai chili sauce

4 to 6 tablespoons olive oil

Put the water and salt in a large container with a lid and stir until the salt has dissolved. Add the chicken tenders to the brine, cover, and refrigerate for 24 hours.

The next day, put the curry, cumin, garlic, yogurt, oil, and pepper in a large bowl and stir until well blended.

Drain the chicken in a colander. Remove the tenders and gently squeeze out the water with your fingers. Add the tenders to the curry mixture, tossing to coat. Set aside.

To make the sauce: Put the pineapple, lime juice, and salt to taste in a food processor. Pulse just until the pineapple is finely chopped, about 6 seconds. Add the chili sauce and process just until combined, about 4 seconds. Do not overprocess the sauce, or it will get too spicy.

Heat 1 tablespoon of the oil in a large skillet over medium heat. Add a few pieces of chicken and cook, turning once, until nicely browned, 3 to 4 minutes per side. Drain on paper towels. Repeat with the remaining oil and chicken, adding more oil to the pan as necessary.

Thread the chicken onto skewers and serve. Put about 2 tablespoons of the sauce in each of six ramekins and serve for dipping.

HANGOVER BRISKET & BISCUIT

These juicy little biscuit sandwiches are perfect bar bites that go well with a cocktail or a glass of wine or beer. Aptly named, they might indeed help cure a hangover. This recipe uses a slow cooker for cooking the brisket. See the Note on page 117 for the oven-roasting method.

SERVES 8 (MAKES 16 SMALL SANDWICHES)

1 tablespoon olive oil

2 small carrots, chopped

6 celery stalks, chopped

$\frac{1}{2}$ medium onion, chopped

One $2\frac{1}{2}$- to 3-pound first-cut brisket, cut into 3 pieces

2 bay leaves

4 fresh thyme sprigs

$1\frac{1}{2}$ cups beef broth

2 tablespoons ketchup

$\frac{1}{3}$ cup tomato juice

1 teaspoon kosher salt

1 teaspoon freshly ground black pepper

4 plum tomatoes, sliced $\frac{1}{4}$ inch thick

2 tablespoons molasses

Homemade Buttermilk Biscuits (recipe follows)

Dijon mustard, for serving

Heat the oil in a large skillet over medium heat and cook the carrots, stirring occasionally, until softened and lightly browned, 5 to 7 minutes. Add the celery and onion and cook for 3 minutes. Add the brisket and sear, turning once, until browned on both sides, about 2 minutes per side. Remove from the heat.

Put the bay leaves and thyme in a slow cooker. Transfer the meat to the slow cooker. Remove the cooked vegetables from the skillet with a slotted spoon and spoon them over the meat. Do not clean the skillet.

Stir the broth, ketchup, and tomato juice together in a small bowl. Pour the mixture into the skillet and bring to a boil. Reduce the heat and simmer, stirring and scraping up the browned bits from the bottom of skillet, until the mixture has reduced by half, about 8 minutes.

Transfer the ketchup mixture to the slow cooker and add the salt and pepper. Turn the cooker on low and cook for 5 hours.

Remove the brisket from the sauce and let cool completely. Strain the sauce through a colander into a bowl, discarding the solids, and let cool completely. If not using the meat and sauce right away, wrap the meat in plastic wrap, transfer the sauce to a container with a lid, and store in the refrigerator for up to 2 days.

Preheat the oven to 375°F.

Arrange the tomato slices in a single layer on a baking sheet. Brush the tops with the molasses. Roast the tomatoes for 6 minutes. Remove and set aside.

Split the biscuits in half, arrange on a baking sheet, and let them warm in the oven for 3 to 5 minutes.

Meanwhile, cut into brisket lengthwise into thirds and then slice crosswise into ⅛-inch-thick slices (approximately 2 by 2-inch slices).

Put the reserved sauce in a large skillet and bring to a simmer. Add the brisket slices and cook, turning once, until heated through, about 2 minutes.

To serve, spread a dab of mustard on the cut side of each biscuit half. Add a slice of brisket to each biscuit half, top each slice with a slice of roasted tomato, and make sandwiches. Pour the sauce remaining from the skillet into a ramekin and serve as a dipping sauce.

Note: To cook the brisket in the oven, preheat the oven to 300°F. Bake the brisket for 3 to 4 hours, basting occasionally with the cooking liquid. Let the meat rest for at least 30 minutes before proceeding with the recipe.

HOMEMADE BUTTERMILK BISCUITS

MAKES ABOUT 16 BISCUITS

2 cups unbleached all-purpose flour

¼ teaspoon baking soda

1 tablespoon kosher salt

6 tablespoons very cold unsalted butter, cut into bits

1 cup buttermilk

1 egg, beaten

Preheat the oven to 450°F.

Put the flour, baking soda, and salt in a food processor. Add the butter and pulse until the mixture resembles coarse meal. Add the buttermilk and pulse until just combined (the dough should be very wet).

Turn the dough out onto a floured work surface. Gently pat out (do not roll out with a rolling pin) the dough to about ½ inch thick. (The secret to the whole process is to handle the dough as little as is possible, or the biscuits will be tough.) Using a biscuit cutter or a glass, cut the dough into 2-inch rounds. Transfer to two baking sheets, arranging them 1 inch apart for "crusty" biscuits or touching each other for softer biscuits. Brush the biscuits with the beaten egg.

Bake until the biscuits are golden brown on the top and bottom, 10 to 12 minutes.

Manhattanite

SERVES 1

2 ounces Rittenhouse rye

1 ounce Dubonnet Rouge

1 teaspoon Cointreau

2 dashes orange bitters

1 orange twist, for garnish

Put the rye, Dubonnet, Cointreau, and bitters in a chilled mixing glass. Add ice, stir, and strain into a chilled cocktail glass. Garnish with the orange twist and serve.

EVENING FALLS

SERVES 1

¾ ounce fresh lemon juice

¼ ounce Simple Syrup (page 16)

¼ ounce Clover Honey Syrup
(recipe follows)

¼ ounce Poire Williams
or other pear eau-de-vie

¼ ounce Luxardo maraschino
liqueur

2 ounces Plymouth gin

2 dashes Scrappy's lavender bitters

Grated cinnamon stick, for garnish

Put the lemon juice, simple syrup, honey syrup, eau-de-vie, maraschino liqueur, gin, and bitters in a cocktail shaker. Add ice, shake, and strain into a chilled cocktail glass. Garnish with cinnamon and serve.

To make the Clover Honey Syrup: Combine equal parts clover honey and boiling water together and stir until the honey is completely dissolved.

FONDA
COMIDA MEXICANA

PARK SLOPE

Although it is sometimes referred to as "Strollerville," Park Slope is a lovely, liveable neighborhood with vast stretches of green space (Prospect Park), streets lined with handsome brownstones and apartment buildings, and scores of good restaurants and bars. Other highlights include community gardens and top-notch farmers' markets.

FONDA

434 7th AVENUE

Chef Roberto Santibañez has been at the forefront of modern Mexican cuisine for many years. He was born in Mexico City, graduated from the Cordon Bleu in Paris, and cooked at highly acclaimed restaurants in Mexico and Austin, Texas, before he became culinary director for the Rosa Mexicano restaurants in Manhattan. In 2009, he opened his own place, Fonda, a lively, authentic Mexican spot in Park Slope. This inviting neighborhood eatery serves gutsy, innovative food and well-crafted cocktails. Appetizers and bar snacks include made-to-order guacamole, flautas, and patatas bravas, and the bar offers signature Margaritas and Palomas as well as sangria, wine, and a wide range of Mexican beers. Based on the success of his Brooklyn outpost, Santibañez has branched out and opened two more Fonda restaurants on the Lower East Side and in Chelsea in Manhattan.

TORTILLA DE HUEVO
MEXICAN-STYLE POTATO FRITTATA

Chef Santibañez serves terrific botanas *(small dishes to share) at Fonda's lively bar. This crispy potato frittata is just the right thing to nibble on with a glass of sangria or a Paloma.*

SERVES 6 TO 8

6 tablespoons olive oil

2 large russet potatoes (about 1 pound), peeled and thinly sliced

Kosher salt

½ white onion, thinly sliced

1 small jalapeño pepper, stemmed, seeded, and chopped

6 large eggs

Heat 3 tablespoons of the oil in an 8-inch nonstick pan over high heat. Add the potatoes and a pinch of salt and stir gently to coat the potatoes evenly. Cover the pan and cook for 3 minutes. Uncover and stir again, turning the potatoes so they will brown evenly. Cover the pan and cook for 4 minutes more.

Add the onion and jalapeño pepper and cook, uncovered, for 7 minutes, stirring frequently to prevent burning. The potatoes should be golden brown and tender. Drain some of the excess oil from the potatoes and let cool slightly.

Lightly beat the eggs in a large bowl with a pinch of salt. Add the potato mixture and gently stir.

Wipe out the pan with paper towels and heat the remaining 3 tablespoons oil over high heat. Pour in the potato-and-egg mixture and scramble briskly for about 1½ minutes, or until the eggs begin to set. Reduce the heat to very low, and tap the pan firmly to release the tortilla. Cook for 5 minutes.

Slide the tortilla onto a lightly oiled plate, then invert it back into the pan and cook until it is lightly browned on the second side and the middle of the tortilla is still soft, 2 to 5 minutes.

Slide the tortilla onto a serving plate and let rest for 5 minutes. Serve whole or cut into wedges.

FONDA HOUSE SANGRIA

SERVES 1

4 ounces full-bodied red wine,
  such as Rioja

½ ounce bourbon

½ ounce triple sec

1 teaspoon fresh lime juice

Slices of fresh oranges
  and peaches, for garnish

Orange zest, for garnish

Pour the wine into a large goblet. Add the bourbon, triple sec, and lime juice and stir. Fill the glass with ice, top with the fruit, garnish with orange zest, and serve.

BROOKLYN SPIRITS

VAN BRUNT STILLHOUSE

Daric Schlesselman, who comes from a long line of Wisconsin farmers, is the founder of Van Brunt Stillhouse. Although he works as a television video editor, he felt the need to produce something more tactile and to get back to his farming roots, so he pursued a passion for distilling. He rented and renovated a large warehouse in Red Hook, turning it into the Van Brunt Stillhouse. It now produces a number of hand-crafted spirits; its growing line of whiskeys includes American, malt, bourbon, rye, and moonshine made with grains that come from upstate New York farms; they also produce Due North rum and Red Hook grappa.

Van Brunt Stillhouse offers weekend tours and features a small bar that serves drinks made from spirits distilled onsite.

VAN BRUNT STILLHOUSE, 6 Bay Street, Brooklyn, NY 11231, www.vanbruntstillhouse.com

LA PALOMA

SERVES 1

Tajín seasoning salt, for rimming the glass (see Note)

1 lime wedge, for rimming the glass

2 ounces mezcal classico

1 ounce passion fruit puree

Jarritos toronja grapefruit soda

1 lime wedge, for garnish

The Paloma (its name means "dove") is a popular drink in Mexico that is rapidly gaining recognition in the States. It's a little bitter and bubbly and very refreshing. Fonda makes its Paloma with mezcal, passion fruit puree, and Jarritos grapefruit soda. If you can't find Jarritos brand, another grapefruit soda such as Squirt or Ting will work well.

Pour the salt onto a small flat plate. Rub the rim of a pint glass with the lime wedge, and dip it into the plate of salt to coat the rim. Fill the glass with ice. Add the mezcal and passion fruit puree, top off with soda, and stir. Garnish with the lime wedge and serve.

Note: Tajín seasoning salt is available in Spanish markets and online.

COBBLE HILL

Cobble Hill is situated between
Carroll Gardens and Brooklyn
Heights. It has both an old-
school charm and a modern
buzz—small mom-and-pop shops
and trendy boutiques line
its streets. This picturesque
neighborhood is home to a wide
variety of excellent, destination-
worthy bars and restaurants.

CLOVER CLUB
NY
210

CLOVER CLUB

210 SMITH STREET

Clover Club is a very special cocktail lounge. From the marble tables and leather booths to the nineteenth-century mahogany bar to the posh back room with a working fireplace, you may think you've stepped into a stylish speakeasy from the Victorian era when you enter it. Co-owner and master mixologist Julie Reiner has been a key player in New York's cocktail scene for many years, and her signature style of using high-quality and fresh market-driven ingredients is evident in Clover Club's finely crafted drinks, both classic and new. The bar menu includes an exquisite quartet of deviled eggs, grilled flatbreads, and more substantial fare like steak frites and decadent mac 'n' cheese.

DEVILED EGG QUARTET

Clover Club's Deviled Egg Quartet is a masterpiece, not a bar food afterthought. Each serving includes four unusual, delectable toppings—Smoked Trout, Smoked Paprika and Bread Crumbs, crispy Bacon Croutons, and creamy Mushroom Duxelles. Paired with a drink or a glass of wine, this is a perfect snack to start off your evening. It would also be lovely to serve at a cocktail party.

MAKES 32 DEVILED EGGS

16 large eggs

1/2 cup mayonnaise

1 tablespoon Dijon mustard

1/2 teaspoon yellow mustard powder

1/2 teaspoon superfine sugar

Kosher salt and freshly ground black pepper

Toppings (recipes follow)

Put the eggs in a large pot and add cold water to cover. Bring just to a gentle boil over medium-high heat, then remove the pot from the heat and cover tightly. Let the eggs stand, covered, for 10 minutes.

Drain the eggs and rinse them under cold water. Pat the eggs dry and let cool completely.

Peel the eggs and cut them lengthwise in half. Gently scoop the yolks into a medium bowl, being careful not to break the whites. Arrange the egg white halves, cavity side up, on a platter and set aside.

Mash the egg yolks with a fork. Stir in the mayonnaise, Dijon and dry mustards, sugar, and salt and pepper to taste and mix until smooth. Add a bit of water if the mixture seems too thick.

Using a small spoon or a piping bag with your preferred tip, mound the filling in the cavities of the egg white halves. (The eggs can be refrigerated for up to 3 hours before serving.)

Sprinkle or spoon the toppings over the eggs before serving.

SMOKED TROUT TOPPING

One 3-ounce smoked trout fillet,
  skin and bones removed
  and flesh crumbled

2 tablespoons crème fraîche

1 tablespoon minced red onion

Freshly ground black pepper

Put the trout, crème fraîche, onion, and pepper to taste in a small bowl and stir together until smooth.

SMOKED PAPRIKA & BREAD CRUMB TOPPING

8 slices white bread, crusts removed

3 tablespoons unsalted butter or olive oil

1 garlic clove, minced

Sweet smoked paprika

Kosher salt and freshly ground black pepper

Preheat the oven to 350°F.

Put the bread in a food processor and pulse until fine.

Heat the butter or oil in a large skillet over medium heat until the butter has melted or the oil is shimmering. Add the garlic and cook for a few seconds until aromatic. Add the bread crumbs and stir until coated.

Spread the bread crumbs onto a baking sheet and bake, stirring occasionally, until golden brown, 5 to 7 minutes. Sprinkle with paprika and salt and pepper to taste, and tossing well.

BACON CROUTON TOPPING

6 slices smoky bacon

1 tablespoon olive oil

Arrange the bacon in two stacks of 3 and cut each stack crosswise into 4 pieces. Put the stacks of bacon in the freezer until firm, about 15 minutes.

Cut the cold bacon into ⅛-inch pieces.

Heat the oil in a large skillet, add the bacon, and cook, stirring occasionally, until crispy. Drain on paper towels.

MUSHROOM DUXELLES TOPPING

8 ounces cremini mushrooms, coarsely chopped

2 tablespoons unsalted butter

2 tablespoons minced shallots

¼ cup dry white wine

¼ cup heavy cream

Kosher salt and freshly ground black pepper

Put the mushrooms in a food processor and pulse until finely chopped, being careful not to overprocess.

Melt the butter in a sauté pan over medium heat. Add the shallots and cook until soft, about 2 minutes. Add the mushrooms and white wine and cook until the pan is nearly dry. Add the cream and simmer until thickened. Add salt and pepper to taste. Remove from the heat.

BROOKLYN SPIRITS

KINGS COUNTY DISTILLERY

Kings County Distillery has the distinction of being New York City's oldest operating whiskey distillery, the first since Prohibition. It was founded in 2010 by Kentucky native Colin Spoelman and is located in the 115-year-old Paymaster Building in the Brooklyn Navy Yard. The distillery produces a distinctive corn whiskey and an aged bourbon. Both have won medals from the ADI Craft Spirit Awards and have received high ratings from numerous publications, including the *New York Times* and *Time Out New York*. In addition, it makes a chocolate whiskey infused with cacao bean husks from the nearby Mast Brothers Chocolate factory. Spoelman and his business partner, David Haskell, are the authors of a very informative book about American whiskey called *A Guide to Urban Moonshining: How to Make and Drink Whiskey*.

Kings County Distillery is open for tours and tastings on Saturdays and recently opened an outdoor whiskey garden.

KINGS COUNTY DISTILLERY, 63 Flushing Avenue, Unit 379, Brooklyn, NY 11205
www.kingscountydistillery.com

POTATO CRISPS

WITH TRUFFLE CRÈME FRAÎCHE

Just like the menu says, "All right, so they are potato chips . . . but they are tossed in duck fat and served with a truffle crème fraîche". Whether you call them crisps or chips, these are heavenly.

SERVES 4 TO 6

Truffle Crème Fraîche:

1 cup crème fraîche

2/3 cup mayonnaise

3 1/2 teaspoons truffle oil

Kosher salt and freshly ground
    black pepper

4 large russet potatoes, peeled

Canola oil, for frying

Fine sea salt

1/4 cup duck fat, melted

Minced fresh chives, for garnish

To make the truffle crème fraîche: Mix the crème fraîche, mayonnaise, truffle oil, and salt and pepper to taste in a small bowl. (The crème fraîche will keep, covered, in the refrigerator for up to a week.)

Using a mandoline, slice the potatoes into thin rounds. Rinse well in cold water. Drain thoroughly and pat dry.

Preheat the oven to 200°F.

Pour 3 inches of canola oil into a heavy-bottomed pan and heat to 350°F over medium-high heat. Working in batches, fry the potatoes until golden brown and crisp, 2 to 3 minutes, and drain on paper towels. Season with sea salt to taste. Add more oil to the pan as needed and heat to 350°F before adding more potatoes. Transfer the crisps to a large metal bowl and keep warm in the oven.

To serve, toss the potato crisps with the melted duck fat to coat. Serve with the truffle crème fraîche, garnished with minced chives.

BACON MAC 'N' CHEESE

Mac 'n' cheese is a bar staple served all over Brooklyn and beyond. This version from Clover Club's Chef Craig Rivard is made with gemelli pasta, but penne, fusilli, or cavatappi work well too. Whether you serve it from a large baking pan or in individual ramekins—as the bar does—this rich and creamy dish is one to savor.

SERVES 6 TO 8

Mornay Sauce:

8 ounces slab bacon,
  cut into medium dice

5 tablespoons unsalted butter

½ yellow onion, chopped

5 garlic cloves, thinly sliced

Kosher salt and freshly ground
  black pepper

5 tablespoons all-purpose flour

2 cups whole milk

2 cups heavy cream

6 ounces Gruyère cheese, grated

6 ounces white Cheddar cheese, grated

Garlic Bread Crumbs:

2 tablespoons unsalted butter

1 garlic clove, finely minced

½ cup panko crumbs or
  fresh white bread crumbs

Kosher salt and freshly ground black pepper

1 pound gemelli, penne, fusilli,
  or cavateppi pasta

4 ounces Gruyère cheese, grated

To make the Mornay sauce: Cook the bacon in a large heavy-bottomed pot until crispy on all sides. Remove the bacon with a slotted spoon and drain on paper towels. Pour the bacon fat into a heatproof bowl and reserve.

Wipe out the pot, add the butter, and melt over medium heat. Add the onion and garlic, reduce the heat, and cook until very soft. Add salt and pepper to taste. Then sprinkle the flour over the onions and stir with a wooden spoon until well coated. Gradually add the milk, whisking until smooth. Repeat with the heavy cream. Bring the sauce to a simmer over medium heat, whisking occasionally, and simmer for 20 minutes.

Whisk in ¼ cup of the reserved bacon fat. Taste and adjust the seasonings if necessary. Turn off the heat and add the cheeses. Using a blender, food processor, or an immersion blender, blend the sauce until very smooth. Set aside.

To make the garlic bread crumbs: Melt the butter in a small skillet over low heat. Add the garlic and stir. Add the bread crumbs and stir to coat. Add salt and pepper to taste and remove from the heat.

Preheat the oven to 400°F.

Cook the pasta according to the package directions; drain.

Reheat the sauce over low heat. Add the cooked pasta and reserved bacon and stir to coat. Pour the pasta into a buttered 2-quart baking dish or six to eight individual ramekins. Top with the bread crumbs and cheese. Bake until the cheese is melted and bubbling and the bread crumbs are lightly browned, 20 to 25 minutes. Serve.

BROOKLYN SPIRITS

GREENHOOK GINSMITHS

Greenhook Ginsmiths is a small artisan distillery based in Greenpoint. It was launched in 2012 by Steven DeAngelo and his brother Philip. DeAngelo was a broker on Wall Street and had no plans to become a gin distiller, but after the recession in 2008, he decided to reevaluate his career. After several years of hard work studying the process of making gin and planning and building a distillery, he developed a rarely used method of vacuum distillation using a copper still. This process removes the air pressure from the still and allows distillation at low temperatures that protect the essence and aroma of the botanicals used in producing gin. This result of this process is a highly aromatic, beautifully flavored gin that has become a favorite of bartenders all over New York.

Greenhook Ginsmiths offers distillery tours and tastings and welcomes gin lovers.

GREENHOOK GINSMITHS, 208 Dupont Street, Brooklyn, NY 11222, www.greenhookgin.com

ROYAL TANNENBAUM

SERVES 1

2 ounces Rittenhouse rye

¾ ounce grapefruit juice

½ ounce Cynar

½ ounce Honey Syrup (see Note)

¼ ounce fresh lemon juice

2 dashes pine tincture (see Note)

1 lemon twist, for garnish

Fill a cocktail shaker with ice. Add the rye, grapefruit juice, Cynar, honey syrup, lemon juice, and pine tincture and shake. Strain into a sour glass, garnish with the lemon twist, and serve.

Note: Honey syrup is made with equal parts honey and boiling water stirred together until the honey is completely dissolved. Pine tincture is available in health food stores and online.

CUZCO

SERVES 1

Kirschwasser, for rinsing the glass

2 ounces Kappa pisco

¾ ounce Aperol

¾ ounce fresh grapefruit juice

½ ounce fresh lemon juice

½ ounce Simple Syrup (page 16)

1 grapefruit twist, for garnish

Rinse a Collins glass with kirschwasser. Combine the pisco, Aperol, grapefruit and lemon juices, and simple syrup in a cocktail shaker. Add ice and shake. Strain into the prepared glass over ice cubes, garnish with the grapefruit twist, and serve.

SOLERA

SERVES 1

1 ounce Calvados

1 ounce Laird's applejack

1 ounce Lustau East India Solera sherry

1 bar spoon Orange Curaçao

2 dashes orange bitters

1 slice or thin round Red Delicious apple, for garnish

Put the Calvados, applejack, sherry, Curaçao, and bitters in a mixing glass. Add ice and stir. Strain into a coupe, garnish with the apple slice, and serve.

NO COUNTRY FOR OLD MEN

SERVES 1

1½ ounces Carpano Antica vermouth

¾ ounce reposado tequila

¾ ounce vida mezcal

¾ ounce fresh lemon juice

½ ounce crème de cacao

1 teaspoon Demerara Simple Syrup (page 17)

Dash of Bittermens Hellfire shrub

Dash of Bittermens Xocolatl Mole bitters

Put the vermouth, tequila, mezcal, lemon juice, crème de cacao, syrup, shrub, and bitters in a cocktail shaker. Add ice and shake. Strain into a cocktail glass and serve.

LONG ISLAND BAR

110 ATLANTIC AVENUE

Barman Toby Cecchini and his business partner, Joel Tompkins, reopened the long-shuttered Long Island Restaurant and Bar in Cobble Hill in 2013. Named one of the Best Bars in America by *Esquire* magazine and highly praised by the New York press, it is a stylish yet easygoing neighborhood haunt that serves no-nonsense drinks and excellent food. In addition to mixing classic and creative house cocktails, Cecchini adds thoughtful homemade touches like marinated cherries for Manhattans and pickled onions to garnish Gibsons. Chef Gabriel Martinez, who cooked at Michelin-starred Alinea in Chicago, sends out fantastic fare such as smoked trout spread, authentic fried cheese curds, and grilled merguez frites and burgers. Look for the original glowing neon sign on the corner of Atlantic Avenue and Henry Street—you can't miss it.

FRIED CHEESE CURDS
WITH "FRENCH ONION DIP"

This dish is an ode to Wisconsin, the home state of the bar's co-owner and head bartender, Toby Cecchini. As all 'Sconies will attest, fried curds are the pinnacle of Midwestern cuisine, and they are served here with pride. These squeaky, cheesy morsels are tossed in a simple beer batter and deep-fried until golden brown. A generous side of creamy onion dip helps cool down the molten nuggets.

SERVES 6

Batter:

¾ cup plus 2 tablespoons all-purpose flour

½ cup cornstarch

2 tablespoons baking powder

1 teaspoon cayenne pepper

1 cup water

1 cup light-bodied beer

12 ounces fresh or frozen cheese curds

French Onion Dip:

1 pound (2 cups) crème fraîche or sour cream

½ cup buttermilk, plus more as needed

1 ounce Thai fried red onion rings (see Note), coarsely chopped

½ ounce Thai fried garlic shavings (see Note)

2 teaspoons kosher salt

½ teaspoon garlic powder

1 tablespoon fresh lemon juice

2 tablespoons minced fresh chives

3 to 4 quarts vegetable oil, for deep-frying

Sea salt

Minced fresh chives, for garnish

To make the batter: Mix the flour, cornstarch, baking powder, and cayenne pepper together in a large bowl. Add the water and beer and whisk until the mixture resembles a thick pancake batter. Add the cheese curds and set aside.

To make the onion dip: Put the crème fraîche, buttermilk, onion rings, garlic shavings, salt, garlic powder, lemon juice, and chives in a bowl and stir together until smooth, adding more buttermilk if the dip seems too thick; it should be slightly thicker than ranch dressing. Cover and refrigerate until needed. (The dip will keep, covered, in the refrigerator for up to 5 days.)

To fry the curds, heat the oil in a large heavy-bottomed pot to 375°F. (The amount of oil is very important; it should be no higher than 4 inches from the top of pot in order to avoid a "boil over" of scorching-hot oil.) When the oil is at 375°F, use one cheese curd as a tester: Gently drop it into the oil to gauge how much bubbling will occur. Fry the curds in small batches until golden brown, 1 to 2 minutes. Remove with a slotted spoon or metal strainer, drain on paper towels, and sprinkle with sea salt and chives. As you fry the cheese curds, the temperature of the oil may drop, so adjust the heat accordingly. (Allow the oil to cool completely before attempting to remove it from the stove.)

Serve the curds with the dip, garnished with chives.

Note: Thai fried red onion rings and garlic shavings can be purchased at Asian grocery stores or online.

RAINBOW CARROT SALAD

Beautiful rainbow carrots have recently been showing up at farmers' markets, and Chef Martinez uses them in this bountiful and refreshing salad—a tangle of vibrant yellow, orange, and purple carrots drizzled with tangy orange vinaigrette, tossed with hunks of sheep's-milk cheese, pickled raisins, capers, piquant chilies, and sunflower sprouts; and topped with fresh herbs and toasted sunflower seeds.

SERVES 6

8 large rainbow or orange carrots, preferably organic

Kosher salt

Orange Vinaigrette:

¼ cup orange vinegar (see Note)

1 tablespoon white vinegar

¼ teaspoon orange blossom water

1 tablespoon honey

¾ cup sunflower oil

½ teaspoon kosher salt

Freshly ground black pepper

Pickled Raisins:

1 cup golden raisins

¾ cup white vinegar

¼ teaspoon orange blossom water

⅓ cup granulated sugar

¼ teaspoon kosher salt

Sunflower Seeds:

1 cup raw sunflower seeds

2 tablespoons sunflower oil

1 teaspoon kosher salt

¼ cup capers, rinsed and drained, for garnish

2 red Fresno peppers, stemmed, seeded, and cut into very thin strips

½ cup sunflower sprouts, trimmed and rinsed

½ cup crumbled sheep's-milk feta cheese, preferably Bulgarian

½ cup chopped fresh dill

½ cup chopped fresh flat-leaf parsley

½ cup chopped fresh tarragon

Using a mandoline, and a healthy amount of caution, shave the carrots lengthwise into thin strips, roughly the thickness of a quarter. You can also do this with a vegetable peeler, making sure to get thick peelings. Transfer the carrots to a large bowl, cover with ice water and add salt to taste. Let the carrots to sit in the ice water in the refrigerator for at least 4 hours; overnight is ideal.

Drain the carrots in a colander and let sit for 10 minutes to remove any excess water.

To make the vinaigrette: Put the orange and white vinegars, orange blossom water, honey, oil, salt, and pepper to taste in a small bowl and whisk together. Set aside.

To make the pickled raisins: Put the raisins in a small bowl. Put the vinegar, orange blossom water, sugar, and salt in a small saucepan and bring to a simmer. Simmer until the salt and sugar have dissolved. Pour over the raisins and let steep until the raisins plump and cool to room temperature, then drain and set aside.

To prepare the sunflower seeds: Preheat the oven to 300°F.

Toss the sunflower seeds with the oil, sprinkle with the salt, and spread on a baking sheet. Bake for 10 minutes. Rotate the pan and bake until the seeds are toasted and golden, 8 to 10 minutes more.

To assemble the salad: Put the carrots, raisins, capers, pepper strips, and sprouts in a large bowl. Add the vinaigrette and toss until well coated.

Transfer to a platter or salad plates, top with the cheese, herbs, and toasted sunflower seeds, and serve.

Note: Orange vinegar can be purchased online at www.sos-chefs.com. Or you can substitute ¼ cup fresh orange juice plus 1 teaspoon white vinegar.

THE ERIN

SERVES 1

2 ounces Evan Williams bourbon

$\frac{1}{2}$ ounce sweet vermouth

$\frac{1}{2}$ ounce Suze or other
gentian liqueur

$\frac{1}{2}$ ounce Bigallet China-China
amer liqueur

5 dashes St. Elizabeth's Allspice
Dram liqueur

2 dashes Angostura bitters

1 orange twist, for garnish

1 lemon twist, for garnish

This cocktail isn't on the menu, but it has become a call by regulars in the cold weather.

Fill a mixing glass with ice. Add the bourbon, vermouth, liqueurs, and bitters and stir with a bar spoon. Strain into a double old-fashioned glass with one large ice cube. Garnish with the orange and lemon twists and serve.

BOULEVARDIER

SERVES 1

1 ounce Rittenhouse rye

1 ounce Old Overholt rye

1 ounce Campari

½ ounce Carpano Antica vermouth

½ ounce Cinzano Rosso vermouth

1 lemon twist, for garnish

The Boulevardier is a variation of a Negroni that is made with whiskey instead of gin. It's a classic cocktail that dates back to the late 1920s and is currently enjoying a comeback. Long Island Bar's excellent Boulevardier is very popular among New York cocktail aficionados.

Fill a mixing glass with ice. Add the ryes, Campari, and vermouths and stir well with a bar spoon. Strain into a chilled coupe or stemmed glass. Garnish with the lemon twist and serve.

"AN APERITIF"

SERVES 1

2 ounces club soda

4 ounces Prosecco

1½ ounces Cappelletti aperitivo

1 green olive, for garnish

1 lemon twist, for garnish

This refreshing aperitif is made with Cappelletti, an artisanal wine-based aperitivo with slightly bitter notes that is made in the Alto Adige region of northern Italy. Mixed with Prosecco and a splash of soda, it is delightful.

Fill a double old-fashioned glass one-third full with ice. Add the soda and Prosecco and top with the Cappelletti. Garnish with the olive and lemon twist and serve.

THE IMPROVED PENDENNIS

SERVES 1

2 ounces Plymouth gin

1 ounce fresh lime juice

¾ ounce Giffard Abricot du Roussillon liqueur

½ ounce Purkhart Blume Marillen apricot eau-de-vie

¼ ounce Simple Syrup (page 16)

3 dashes Peychaud's bitters

This is bartender Toby Cecchini's citrusy version of the Pendennis Club Cocktail, a classic that was invented in the 1880s at the Pendennis Club in Louisville, Kentucky.

Fill a cocktail shaker with ice. Add the gin, lime juice, apricot liqueur, eau-de-vie, simple syrup, and bitters and shake vigorously. Strain into a chilled coupe or stemmed glass.

HENRY PUBLIC

329 HENRY STREET

Located on bucolic Henry Street, Henry Public has an antiquey ambience, and the bar features both old-fashioned and reimagined cocktails, like the Kings County Sour and the absinthe-laced Brooklyn Ferry. Its small, well-edited menu offers oysters, pickles, deviled eggs, turkey leg sandwiches, "hamburger sandwiches," and roasted beef marrow bones. For dessert, there are Wilkinsons, a version of Danish *ebelskivers,* with rum-caramel sauce. The young crowd and local families alike eat and drink in wooden booths opposite the zinc-topped bar or in a small back room that has a working fireplace.

BEEF MARROW BONES
WITH WATERCRESS GREMOLATA

Spreading warm, rich bone marrow onto grilled bread is a real treat, and roasted bone marrow is a specialty at Henry Public. Marrow bones are the shank bones of beef; when buying them, ask your butcher to cut them lengthwise in half. The Watercress Gremolata is a wonderful accompaniment, as it offsets the richness of the marrow.

SERVES 8

8 beef marrow bones, halved lengthwise and cut into 3- to 4-inch pieces by the butcher

Watercress Gremolata:
$1/3$ cup coarsely chopped watercress
$1/3$ cup coarsely chopped fresh flat-leaf parsley

$1/3$ cup thinly sliced shallots
Juice of 1 lemon
Kosher salt and freshly ground black pepper

Coarse sea salt
Toasted or grilled bread, for serving

Preheat the oven to 450°F.

Arrange the bones, marrow-side up, on a baking sheet and roast until the marrow is soft and nearly ready to slide out but not melting away, about 10 minutes.

Meanwhile, make the gremolata: Combine the watercress, parsley, and shallots in a small bowl. Toss with enough of the lemon juice to lightly coat. Season to taste with salt and pepper.

Top each marrow bone with gremolata and a sprinkle of sea salt. Serve with grilled bread.

JUNIPER PICKLES

The pickle plate is a staple of bars all over Brooklyn, and with good reason. Briny and crunchy, sweet and sour, pickles are the perfect foil for the rich fare featured on so many bar menus. This recipe from Henry Public is easy to make. Having a few jars of homemade pickles will always come in handy—layer them on sandwiches, serve with hot dogs and burgers, or add to a platter of assorted cheeses and charcuterie.

MAKES ABOUT 1 PINT

1 pound Kirby cucumbers, sliced ¼ inch thick

1 cup distilled white vinegar

½ cup water

⅓ cup granulated sugar

1 red Thai bird chili

1½ teaspoons black peppercorns

1½ teaspoons mustard seeds

1½ teaspoons juniper berries

½ teaspoon kosher salt

Put the cucumber slices in a large bowl.

Put the vinegar, water, sugar, chili, peppercorns, mustard seeds, juniper berries, and salt in a large saucepan and bring to a boil. Reduce the heat and simmer for 5 minutes. Remove from the heat and let stand for 5 minutes. Pour the vinegar mixture over the cucumbers and let cool to room temperature, then transfer to an airtight container and refrigerate for at least 12 to 24 hours before serving. The pickles will keep, covered, in the refrigerator for up to a week.

cocktails

KINGS COUNTY SOUR

SERVES 1

1 large egg white

¾ ounce fresh lemon juice

1 bar spoon granulated sugar

2 ounces Old Overholt rye

Port

1 orange half-wheel, for garnish

1 maraschino cherry, for garnish

Put the egg white, lemon juice, sugar, and rye in a cocktail shaker and shake. Add ice and shake again. Strain into a rocks glass filled with ice. Float the port on top. Garnish with the orange wheel and cherry and serve.

BROOKLYN HEIGHTS
Brooklyn Heights, which has been on the National Register of Historic Places since 1966, is a beautiful neighborhood noted for its tree-lined streets with gracious row houses, stately churches, and breathtaking views from the Brooklyn Promenade.

COLONIE

127 ATLANTIC AVENUE

Located on the edge of the Brooklyn Heights neighborhood, Colonie is a smart, well-run establishment that serves imaginative cocktails and delicious farm-to-table food. This handsome, casual space, complemented by a large wall garden and an open kitchen, is warm and inviting. The bar in front is a perfect spot to sip an Empire State Sour, a drink made with American whiskey and juiced organic apples, and order a bite to eat from the seasonal menu that includes oysters, crostini, assorted cheeses, salads, and small plates.

COLONIE

RICOTTA CROSTINI

This luscious appetizer has been served at Colonie since the day it opened. The light and creamy fresh ricotta needs just a touch of lemon zest and fresh pepper.

SERVES 4 TO 6

1 pint fresh ricotta cheese,
   at room temperature (see Note)

1 teaspoon grated lemon zest

2 teaspoons sea salt

Freshly ground black pepper

6 thick slices sourdough bread

1 to 2 teaspoons honey

6 fresh mint leaves, torn in half

Gently mix the cheese, lemon zest, salt, and pepper to taste in a large bowl until smooth.

Grill or toast the bread until golden brown.

To serve, spoon some of the ricotta mixture onto each toast and cut in half on an angle. Drizzle the toasts with a bit of honey and garnish each with half a mint leaf.

Note: Colonie uses Salvatore Brooklyn ricotta cheese, but any creamy ricotta will work.

WAX BEAN SALAD
WITH CANDIED GARLIC & SOY MARINADE

The kitchen larder at Colonie is always stocked with as many made-from-scratch pantry staples as possible. Chef Andrew Whitcomb says, "We make jams, jellies, preserves, vinegars, pickles, and condiments all the time. It's very important for me to have these items on hand, because I never know what will spark a bit of inspiration." This delicious salad, served at the bar, is full of crunch and salty-sour flavor that comes from two of their house-made specialties, Candied Garlic and Soy Marinade.

SERVES 4 TO 6

1 pound mixed green, yellow, and purple wax beans, trimmed and cut into 3-inch pieces

3 tablespoons salt

2 tablespoons Candied Garlic (recipe follows)

3 tablespoons Soy Marinade (recipe follows)

¼ cup grated fresh horseradish, for serving

5 chive flowers, chopped, for serving

Bring a large pot of salted water to a boil. Add the beans in batches, making sure that the water doesn't stop boiling, and cook for about 45 seconds, then remove with a skimmer and transfer to a bowl of ice water. Drain the beans thoroughly.

To serve, toss the beans with the candied garlic and the soy marinade. Taste and adjust the seasonings. Arrange the beans on salad plates and top with the horseradish and chive flowers.

CANDIED GARLIC

"I use this on a lot of different dishes to finish. It gives a beautiful garlic flavor, without being crazy harsh. Although two quarts of oil may sound excessive, it is needed to fry the garlic properly, and as a flavor bonus, we save the garlic oil and use it in the restaurant regularly," says Chef Whitcomb.

MAKES ABOUT ½ CUP

5 heads garlic, peeled, separated into cloves, and trimmed

2 quarts canola oil

1 tablespoon powdered sugar

Put the garlic in a food processor and process until coarsely chopped. Transfer the garlic to a clean kitchen towel, wrap it in the towel, and wring out any excess moisture.

Heat the oil in a large heavy-bottomed pot over medium-high heat. Add the garlic and fry, stirring constantly, until golden brown, about 10 minutes. Strain the garlic oil through a fine-mesh sieve into a bowl. Transfer the garlic to a baking sheet lined with paper towels and pat dry. Reserve the garlic oil for other uses.

Sprinkle the garlic with the powdered sugar and toss gently to coat. Store the candied garlic in an airtight container for up to a week.

SOY MARINADE

This fabulous soy marinade is Colonie's version of ponzu, a citrus-based sauce prevalent in Japanese cuisine. The kitchen uses it as a marinade for fish, chicken, or beef, but it really shines when tossed with fresh vegetables or salads.

MAKES ABOUT 1 PINT

Grated zest and juice of 3 limes

Grated zest and juice of 2 lemons

Grated zest and juice of 1 orange

½ cup red wine vinegar

3 tablespoons soy sauce

2 tablespoons fish sauce

2 tablespoons extra-virgin olive oil

1 tablespoon sesame oil

2 tablespoons honey

½ cup finely chopped fresh cilantro

½ cup thinly sliced scallions

Put the citrus zests and juices, vinegar, soy and fish sauces, olive and sesame oils, and honey in a blender and blend until emulsified. Transfer to a bowl, add the cilantro and scallions, and whisk together. The marinade will keep in the refrigerator for about a week.

COOL HAND CUKE

SERVES 1

1½ ounces Crop cucumber vodka

½ ounce St-Germain elderflower liqueur

2 ounces fresh cucumber juice

½ ounce fresh lime juice

½ ounce Mint Simple Syrup (recipe follows)

1 cucumber slice, for garnish

Mint Simple Syrup:

2 cups granulated sugar

2 cups water

1 bunch fresh mint, trimmed

Fill a cocktail shaker with ice, add the vodka, elderflower liqueur, cucumber and lime juices, and simple syrup, and shake vigorously. Strain the drink into a martini glass. Slide the cucumber slice onto a skewer, garnish the drink with it, and serve.

To make the Mint Simple Syrup: Combine the sugar and water in a heavy-bottomed saucepan, and bring to a gentle boil over medium heat, stirring to dissolve the sugar. Remove from the heat, add the mint, and let steep for 15 minutes.

Strain the syrup into a clean container with a lid, cover, and refrigerate until ready to use. The syrup will keep in the refrigerator for up to a month.

EMPIRE STATE SOUR

SERVES 1

2 ounces rye whiskey

1 ounce fresh lemon juice

½ ounce Simple Syrup (page 16)

½ Granny Smith apple, juiced

1 teaspoon egg white

2 dashes Bar Keep baked
apple bitters

Pinch of ground cinnamon,
for garnish

1 cinnamon stick, for garnish

Fill a cocktail shaker with the whiskey, lemon juice, simple syrup, apple juice, egg white, and bitters and shake vigorously. Strain the drink into a rocks glass. Dust with cinnamon, garnish with the cinnamon stick, and serve.

GRAN ELECTRICA

5 FRONT STREET

Gran Electrica, a lively spot, serves diverse, market-driven Mexican fare made with authentic ingredients like fresh tortillas, house-made crema and queso fresco, and spicy chorizo. It is the creation of Colonie partners Tamer Hamawi, Emelie Kihlstrom, and Elise Rosenberg. Mexican-inspired cocktails created by Hamawi, the beverage director, are crafted with a range of tequilas and mezcals made by small-batch distillers. When the weather is balmy, there are few finer places in the city to drink and dine than the lovely expansive outdoor garden, which boasts a great view of the Brooklyn Bridge.

LIFES
TOO SHORT
TO DRINK
BAD
TEQUILA

TOSTADA JAIBA

These beautiful, delicate crab tostadas are served at the bar and as an appetizer at Gran Electrica. The restaurant is lucky enough to have an in-house mother-daughter team making fresh tortillas every day, but this can be made with any good corn tortillas.

SERVES 4 TO 6

2 pounds peekytoe crabmeat
  (from the legs only)

1 habanero pepper, stemmed,
  seeded, and finely diced

1 small white onion, finely diced

1 fresh orange segment, finely diced

1 fresh grapefruit segment, finely diced

½ cup finely chopped fresh cilantro

¼ cup fresh lime juice

¼ cup fresh orange juice

¼ cup fresh grapefruit juice

2 tablespoons extra-virgin olive oil

Vegetable oil, for shallow-frying

12 small corn tortillas
  (about 4 inches in diameter; see Note)

Put the crabmeat, pepper, onion, and diced orange and grapefruit in a large bowl, add ¼ cup of the cilantro, and gently toss together. Add the lime, orange, and grapefruit juices and olive oil and gently toss again, being careful not to break up the crabmeat too much.

Heat 1 tablespoon of the vegetable oil in a large heavy-bottomed pot until hot but not smoking. Fry the tortillas until golden brown, about 2 minutes per side. Add more oil, as needed. Drain on paper towels. Continue frying the remaining tortillas.

To serve, spoon the crabmeat mixture onto the tortillas and garnish with the remaining ¼ cup cilantro.

Note: Hot Bread Kitchen makes excellent small corn tortillas. Their retail location is at 1590 Park Avenue, and they sell their products at greenmarkets throughout New York and online.

GUACAMOLE

The secret ingredient in Gran Electrica's guacamole is dried avocado leaves, which come from native avocado plants grown in Mexico. Available at Mexican specialty stores and online, they add a nice anise taste to the mix.

SERVES 4 TO 6

Leaves from 1 bunch cilantro, chopped

1 medium white onion, coarsely chopped

1 garlic clove

2 jalapeño peppers, stemmed, seeded, and chopped

2 tablespoons dried Mexican avocado leaves

3 tablespoons fresh lime juice

1 teaspoon kosher salt

6 ripe avocados, halved, pitted, peeled, and coarsely chopped

Corn tortilla chips, for serving

Put the cilantro, onion, garlic, jalapeños, and avocado leaves in a blender and blend to a smooth puree. Add the lime juice and salt and blend again.

Mash the avocados with a fork in a large bowl until the consistency is a coarse chunky puree. Add the cilantro puree and mash again. Taste and adjust the seasonings if necessary. Serve with corn chips.

ELOTE

MEXICAN CORN WITH CHIPOTLE MAYONNAISE

Grilled fresh corn slathered with spicy mayonnaise and cheese is a bar favorite at Gran Electrica. What could go better with a Margarita?

SERVES 4 TO 6

6 ears fresh sweet corn in the husk

¼ cup mayonnaise

2 teaspoons chipotle paste

Fresh lime juice

Pinch of kosher salt

2 cups crumbled cotija cheese, for dusting

½ cup ground chile piquín, for serving

Lime wedges, for serving

Preheat the oven to 400°F.

Soak the corn, in its husks, in a large bowl of water for 10 minutes.

Remove the corn from the water and wrap each ear in aluminum foil. Roast the corn for 45 minutes.

Meanwhile, stir the mayonnaise and chipotle paste together in a bowl. Add lime juice and salt to taste.

Unwrap the corn and remove the husks, leaving the stalk ends intact so you have something to hold on to. Brush each ear of warm corn with the chipotle mayo, roll in the cotija cheese to coat, and dust with chile piquín. Serve with lime wedges.

MARGARITA DE TORONJA PICANTE

SERVES 1

Chile piquín salt, for rimming the glass

Fresh grapefruit juice,
   for rimming the glass

1½ ounces habanero-infused
   Pueblo Viejo blanco tequila
   (see Note)

½ ounce triple sec, preferably Combier

1 ounce fresh lime juice

1 ounce fresh grapefruit juice

½ ounce Jalapeño Simple Syrup
   (recipe follows)

1 grapefruit round, for garnish

Jalapeño Simple Syrup:
MAKES ABOUT 2 CUPS

2 cups granulated sugar

2 cups water

2 small jalapeño peppers,
   cut lengthwise in half and seeded

Pour the salt onto a small flat plate. Moisten the rim of a rocks glass with grapefruit juice and dip it into the plate of salt to coat the rim.

Put the tequila, triple sec, lime and grapefruit juices, and jalapeño syrup in a cocktail shaker. Add ice and shake vigorously. Strain into an ice-filled rocks glass. Garnish with the grapefruit round and serve.

To make the Jalapeño Simple Syrup:
Combine the sugar and water in a heavy-bottomed saucepan and bring to a gentle boil over medium heat, stirring to dissolve the sugar. Remove from the heat, add the peppers, and let sit overnight. Strain the syrup into a clean container with a tight-fitting lid and refrigerate until ready to use. The syrup will keep in the refrigerator for up to a month.

Note: To make infused tequila, add 1 stemmed, seeded, and quartered habanero pepper to a 750-ml bottle of blanco tequila.

MI MICHELADA

SERVES 1

Celery salt, for rimming the glass

Chile piquín salt,
   for rimming the glass

6 dashes Valentina
   or other hot sauce

4 dashes Worcestershire sauce

2 ounces Clamato juice

1 ounce fresh lime juice

One 12-ounce can Tecate beer

1 long cucumber spear,
   for garnish

Combine the celery and piquín salts on a small, flat plate. Dip a chilled pint glass into the plate to coat the rim of the glass, then coat the inside of the glass with the hot sauce and fill with ice cubes. Add the Worcestershire sauce, Clamato, and lime juice. Stir and top off with beer. Garnish with the cucumber spear and serve with the remaining beer for topping off as you drink it.

FORT DEFIANCE

365 VAN BRUNT STREET

Getting to Red Hook can be a bit of a challenge, but it's definitely worth the trip if you visit Fort Defiance. Writer and owner St. John Frizell opened this café/bar/restaurant in 2009 after learning the art of bartending at Pegu Club. The bar at this unpretentious joint serves a superlative New Orleans–inspired Sazerac (Frizell lived there for many years), a King Bee made with tea-infused vodka, and a perfect martini. Winter drinks include a bracing Irish Coffee and a Hot Apple Toddy. On the menu are delectable dishes for pairing with drinks, among them oysters on the half-shell, creamy deviled eggs with fried capers, a muffuletta sandwich (New Orleans again), and a luscious chicken liver pâté served with bacon-onion jam and a stack of perfectly grilled toasts.

RED HOOK

Red Hook, a formerly rough-and-tumble waterfront neighborhood, has a small-town feel. Despite the presence of some big box stores and vast warehouses, it is also home to a number of small residential enclaves and artisanal shops and businesses developed by urban pioneers and creative entrepreneurs. It was once one of the country's busiest shipping centers, and the sweeping views of New York Bay, the Statue of Liberty, and lower Manhattan are spectacular.

MUFFULETTA

Showing its New Orleans influences, Fort Defiance serves the most authentic muffuletta in the city. This iconic sandwich is made with a big round loaf of bread, filled with Italian meats, cheese, and olive salad and cut into wedges for serving. Fort Defiance's version includes a healthy portion of olive salad, made with house-made pickled vegetables, olives, and capers. The salad can also be served as a savory condiment to accompany other dishes.

SERVES 6 TO 8

Olive Salad:

1 head cauliflower, trimmed and cut into small pieces

1 pound carrots, peeled and finely diced

1 pound red bell peppers, cored, seeded, and finely diced

1 bunch celery, trimmed and diced

6 cups water

5 cups white wine vinegar

1 cup dry white wine

2¼ cups granulated sugar

¼ cup kosher salt

1 tablespoon freshly ground black pepper

1½ teaspoons fennel seeds

1 cinnamon stick

3 garlic cloves

3 fresh rosemary sprigs

3 fresh thyme sprigs

3 bay leaves

1 teaspoon red pepper flakes

1½ pounds pitted kalamata olives, chopped

1½ pounds Spanish olives, chopped

¼ cup capers

1 round loaf crusty Italian bread (8 to 9 inches in diameter)

2 tablespoons olive oil

10 slices salami (see Note)

8 slices capicola

5 slices mortadella

5 slices provolone

To make the olive salad: Put the chopped vegetables in a large clean heatproof container. Put the water, vinegar, wine, sugar, salt, black pepper, fennel seeds, cinnamon stick, garlic, rosemary, thyme, bay leaves, and red pepper flakes in a large pot and bring to a boil. Pour the boiling brine over the vegetables. Cover and brine in the refrigerator for 2 days.

Drain the vegetables and transfer to a large bowl. Add the olives and capers and stir well. Cover and refrigerate until ready to serve.

To assemble the sandwich, split the bread in half and dress each half with the olive oil and a generous amount of olive salad. Layer the salami, capicola, mortadella, and provolone on the bottom half of the bread. Press the sandwich halves together and let it sit for an hour or two before serving. Slice the muffuletta into 6 to 8 wedges and serve.

Note: Fort Defiance uses Fra' Mani Salame Toscano from Fra' Mani Handcrafted Foods. Its products are available at gourmet markets and online.

CHICKEN LIVER PÂTÉ
WITH BACON-ONION JAM

This smooth and silky pâté is easy to make and inexpensive, but it tastes luxurious. Serve with toasts or crackers for a cocktail party or as a sandwich spread. The savory jam is a blend of slow-cooked caramelized onions, diced bacon, brown sugar, and balsamic vinegar.

SERVES 6 TO 8

8 tablespoons (1 stick) unsalted butter, cut into cubes, at room temperature

2 shallots, finely chopped

1 pound chicken livers, trimmed

1 tablespoon chopped fresh thyme

⅓ cup Madeira or port

3 tablespoons heavy cream, plus more if needed

Kosher salt

Grilled bread, for serving

Bacon-Onion Jam (recipe follows), for serving

In a large sauté pan over medium heat, melt 4 tablespoons of the butter until it begins to foam. Add the shallots and sauté until translucent, making sure they don't brown. Add the livers, thyme, and Madeira and raise the heat. Cook, stirring occasionally, until the wine has reduced and the livers are lightly browned but still soft and pink on the inside, about 5 minutes.

Remove from the heat and transfer to a blender or food processor. Add the cream, the remaining 4 tablespoons butter, and salt to taste and blend until smooth, adding a little more cream, if necessary. Taste and adjust the seasonings, if necessary. Pack the pâté into a jar or bowl and smooth the top with a spatula or knife. Cover with plastic wrap and refrigerate until firm, about 2 hours or up to 5 days.

Serve the pâté with grilled bread and bacon-onion jam.

BACON-ONION JAM

12 ounces slab bacon, diced
4 white onions, chopped
1½ teaspoons mustard seeds
2½ tablespoons brown sugar
¼ cup balsamic vinegar
3 tablespoons water
Kosher salt and freshly ground black pepper

Heat a heavy pot over medium heat. Add the bacon and cook, stirring occasionally, until the fat has completely rendered and the bacon has begun to crisp, about 12 minutes.

Drain off all but 1 tablespoon of the fat from the pot and add the onions, mustard seeds, brown sugar, vinegar, and water; stir to combine, cover, reduce the heat to very low, and cook undisturbed for 15 minutes.

Remove the lid, stir again, and partially cover the pot. Cook until most of the liquid is gone and the onions are dark and thickened, about 1 hour; add a bit more water if necessary as the jam cooks. Add salt and pepper to taste.

Remove the jam from the heat and let cool slightly. Spoon into a jar or bowl and let cool completely. The jam will keep, covered, in the refrigerator for up to a week.

KING BEE

SERVES 1

1½ ounces Infused Vodka
   (recipe follows)

½ ounce fresh lemon juice

½ ounce Simple Syrup (page 16)

Sparkling wine

1 butterflied lemon slice, for garnish

Infused Vodka:

MAKES 12 OUNCES

1½ cups vodka

3 tablespoons loose black tea

1½ ounces Bénédictine

8 dashes Angostura bitters

The base of this drink is vodka infused with tea, Bénédictine, and bitters. Frizell says, "We use Comb vodka, made in Port Chester, New York, from pure honey—hence the name. Since Bénédictine is expensive, look for a small bottle (unless you really like to drink it). You can make this recipe without it, but it's the ingredient that really makes the drink great."

Fill a cocktail shaker with ice. Add the vodka, lemon juice, and simple syrup and shake. Strain into an ice-filled rocks glass. Top off with sparkling wine, garnish with the lemon slice, and serve.

To make the Infused Vodka: Combine the vodka, tea, Bénédictine, and bitters in a bowl or other container and let steep for 15 minutes, no more. Strain into a clean quart container.

ST. JOHN'S MARTINI

SERVES 1

2¼ ounces Plymouth gin

¾ ounce Dolin dry vermouth

1 dash Angostura orange bitters

1 lemon twist, for garnish

Fill a mixing glass with ice. Add the gin, vermouth, and bitters and stir. Strain into a chilled martini glass. Garnish with the lemon twist and serve.

MORE BROOKLYN BAR BITES

As any restaurateur or barkeep will attest, running an establishment in New York City can be a very challenging endeavor. Circumstances like the ever-changing real-estate landscape (higher rents), a fluctuating service economy, and even a spate of bad weather can cause a business to fold no matter how much hard work and dedication is put into it. During the production of this book, a few of the places we worked with closed for a number of different reasons. They may be gone, but their wonderful recipes for bar food and cocktails live on. Cheers to all these late, great spots!

CRISPY PIMENTO CHEESE
WITH GREEN TOMATO CHOW-CHOW

Kyle Knall was the chef at Char No. 4, where he showcased his deep Southern roots and served classics like this one.

MAKES ABOUT 2 DOZEN BITES

4 cups grated Cheddar cheese

8 ounces cream cheese, softened

1/3 cup jarred pimentos, drained, seeded, and diced

1 1/2 teaspoons paprika

1/2 teaspoon cayenne pepper

1/2 teaspoon yellow mustard powder

4 dashes Tabasco sauce

Kosher salt and freshly ground black pepper

1 cup all-purpose flour

1 cup panko bread crumbs

2 large eggs

Vegetable, corn, or peanut oil, for deep-frying

Green Tomato Chow-Chow (recipe follows), for serving

Put the Cheddar cheese, cream cheese, pimentos, paprika, cayenne pepper, mustard powder, Tabasco sauce, and salt and black pepper to taste in a large bowl. Mix together with your hands until well combined. Roll the mixture into a log, wrap in plastic wrap, and freeze for up to 2 hours.

Put the flour and panko in two separate shallow bowls. Beat the eggs in another shallow bowl.

Slice the cheese roll into 1-inch rounds with a bread knife. Dip each round in the flour, eggs, and then the panko until well coated and transfer to a parchment paper-lined baking sheet.

Pour 3 inches of oil into a deep heavy-bottomed saucepan and heat the oil to 350°F over medium heat. Working in batches, fry the rounds until golden brown, 2 to 3 minutes. Transfer to a plate lined with paper towels.

Serve warm, with the chow-chow.

GREEN TOMATO CHOW-CHOW

MAKES 2½ PINTS

6 green tomatoes, cored
and finely chopped

2 green bell peppers, cored, seeded,
and finely chopped

1 red bell pepper, cored, seeded,
and finely chopped

2 onions, finely chopped

1 tablespoon yellow mustard seeds

1½ teaspoons celery seeds

1 cup cider vinegar

1 cup granulated sugar

1 tablespoon kosher salt

Put the tomatoes, peppers, onions, mustard seeds, celery seeds, vinegar, sugar, and salt in a large nonreactive pot, stir well, and bring to a boil. Reduce the heat and simmer for 25 minutes. Let cool.

Transfer the chow-chow to a clean glass container. It will keep, covered, in the refrigerator for up to a month.

SMOKED CHICKEN WINGS
WITH ALABAMA WHITE SAUCE

You can make smoked chicken wings at home using a gas grill with a smoker box, or cook them over indirect heat in a charcoal grill. Alternatively, bake the chicken wings in the oven and finish them under the broiler.

SERVES 6 TO 8

Dry Rub:

2 tablespoons garlic powder

1 tablespoon onion powder

1 teaspoon cayenne pepper

1 tablespoon dried oregano

2 tablespoons brown sugar

1 tablespoon kosher salt

1 tablespoon freshly ground black pepper

4 pounds chicken wings

Extra-virgin olive oil, for serving

Sea salt

Alabama White Sauce (recipe follows),
   for serving

To make the rub: Mix the garlic powder, onion powder, cayenne pepper, oregano, brown sugar, kosher salt, and black pepper together in a large bowl. Add the chicken wings and stir and turn to coat well. Cover and let marinate in the refrigerator overnight or for at least 2 hours.

Grill Method: Preheat a gas grill with a smoker box or prepare a charcoal fire for indirect/medium-low heat.

Put the wings in the center of the grill grate over indirect heat. Cover and grill, turning the wings every 10 minutes, until they are slightly crispy and completely cooked through, about 30 to 35 minutes.

Oven Method: Preheat the oven to 375°F.

Arrange the wings on a rack set over a baking sheet. Bake for 45 minutes, turning every 15 minutes. Remove the wings and preheat the broiler. Broil the wings until browned and crispy, 5 to 10 minutes.

Arrange the wings on a large platter. Brush with olive oil, sprinkle with sea salt, and serve with the sauce.

ALABAMA WHITE SAUCE

At many barbecue joints in the South, this is the sauce of choice to accompany barbecued ribs, chicken, and pulled pork. It also makes a fine dip for French fries or potato chips.

MAKES ABOUT 1 CUP

¾ cup mayonnaise

2 tablespoons cider vinegar

2 teaspoons prepared horseradish

Dash of Tabasco sauce

Kosher salt and freshly ground black pepper

Whisk the mayonnaise, vinegar, horseradish, Tabasco sauce, and salt and pepper to taste in a medium bowl. The sauce will keep, covered, in the refrigerator for up to 2 weeks.

cocktail

NOR'EASTER

SERVES 1

2 ounces bourbon

½ ounce fresh lime juice

½ ounce maple syrup

1½ ounces ginger beer

1 fresh lime wheel, for garnish

Fill a cocktail shaker with ice. Add the bourbon, lime juice, and maple syrup and shake vigorously for 20 seconds. Strain into an ice-filled rocks glass. Top off with the ginger beer, garnish with the lime wheel, and serve.

CRAFT-BREWED CHURROS

Spirited, a lovely spot in Prospect Heights, was the brainchild of "baketender" Kimberly Wetherell. Craft cocktails and dessert pairings were the centerpiece of the Spirited menu, and churros made with a lager batter pair beautifully with The Holy Mole (page 185).

MAKES 6 TO 8 CHURROS

Churro Batter:

3 tablespoons plus 1 teaspoon
  powdered milk

1¼ cups Brooklyn Lager
  or other favorite beer

4 tablespoons unsalted butter

¼ cup granulated sugar

1 tablespoon kosher salt

1 cup plus 2 tablespoons
  all-purpose flour

2 large eggs

2 quarts vegetable oil or shortening,
  for deep-frying

¾ cup granulated sugar

¼ cup bourbon-smoked sugar
  (see Note, page 184)

1 teaspoon ground cinnamon

To make the batter: Put the powdered milk in a mixing bowl. Slowly add the beer, being careful that it doesn't create an enormous head, and whisk together. Set aside until the foam settles, 2 to 3 minutes.

Transfer the beer mixture to a medium saucepan. Add the butter, sugar, and salt and cook over medium heat until the butter has melted and the mixture begins to simmer. Quickly add all the flour and stir vigorously with a wooden spoon until a sticky dough forms and there is a light film on the bottom of the pan. Remove from the heat, cover, and let the batter rest for 15 minutes.

Stir the eggs into the batter one at a time, making sure each egg is fully incorporated before adding the next. Once the dough is smooth and slightly gloopy (there really is no other word for it), transfer it to a bowl and press a length of plastic wrap tightly against the top of the dough to create an airtight seal. Chill the dough in the refrigerator for at least 4 hours.

Fit a pastry bag with a star tip (such as Atecco 824) and fill it with the chilled batter.

Heat the oil to 375°F in a large heavy-bottomed pot. Holding the pastry tip just above the surface of the hot oil, gently pipe 4-inch lengths of the dough into the pot, without crowding, cutting the dough away from pastry tip with kitchen shears or a sharp knife. Fry the churros, turning often with a spider, slotted spoon, or tongs to ensure that all sides are deep golden brown, for 2 to 3 minutes for a slightly soft center, or 4 to 5 minutes for a crunchier texture. Transfer the churros to a rack set over a baking sheet to allow the excess oil to drip off and the churros to cool slightly.

Meanwhile, mix the sugars and cinnamon together until well combined and spread out on a plate or in a shallow bowl. Roll each magical fried-dough beer stick in the sugar mixture to coat evenly. Serve warm, with your favorite sauce or honey, if desired.

Note: Bourbon-smoked sugar is available online at www.bourbonbarrelfoods.com.

THE HOLY MOLE

SERVES 1

1½ ounces Maker's Mark bourbon

1 ounce Amaro Montenegro

1 teaspoon Tempus Fugit
or other crème de cacao

2 dashes Bitterman's Xocolatl
Mole bitters

1 dash Angostura bitters

Put the bourbon, amaro, crème de cacao, and bitters in a mixing glass. Add ice to fill and stir for 15 to 20 seconds to chill and dilute. Strain the drink into a chilled cocktail glass and serve straight up.

THE BEAST

SERVES 1

1½ ounces Greenhook Ginsmiths
American dry gin

¾ ounce Lillet rosé

½ ounce Campari

1 teaspoon Luxardo
maraschino liqueur

1 dash Angostura orange bitters

1 twist of orange peel, for garnish

Put the gin, Lillet, Campari, liqueur, and bitters in a mixing glass. Add ice to fill and stir quickly for 15 to 20 seconds to chill and dilute the drink. Strain into a chilled rocks glass over two ice cubes. Twist the orange peel to express the oil over the cocktail, then rub the orange peel around the lip of the glass to perfume it, add to the drink as a garnish, and serve.

ACKNOWLEDGMENTS

My thanks and gratitude go out to the many people who worked with me on this book:

The people at Rizzoli, publisher Charles Miers for believing in this book; my editor, Sandy Gilbert Freidus, for her smart suggestions and editing skills and for keeping the book on track; Kayleigh Jankowski for her great production work and her patience; Judith Sutton and Ivy McFadden for their keen-eyed copyediting and food savvy.

Ethan Fixell, for contributing his invaluable expertise on all things beer and Brooklyn.

Angela Miller, my agent, who did what she always does best—she made this book happen.

Jennifer May, for her great photography, brilliant eye, and intrepid approach to shooting under any circumstances, and Caitlin Frackelton for her invaluable assistance on our excellent adventure.

The many Brooklyn restaurateurs, chefs, and bartenders and their staffs who welcomed us into their places and shared their stories and recipes and their wonderful food and drinks. I am in awe of their grit, talent, and generosity and am privileged to know them.

My husband and Uber driver, Lester, and our daughters, Zan and Isabelle, for always being there for me and for everything else.

Index

Page numbers in *italics* indicate illustrations.

First published in the United States of America in 2016
by Rizzoli International Publications, Inc.
300 Park Avenue South
New York, New York 10010
www.rizzoliusa.com

2016 2017 2018 2019 / 10 9 8 7 6 5 4 3 2 1

Printed in China

ISBN 13: 978-0-8478-4825-6

Library of Congress Control Number: 2015958265

Project Editor: Sandra Gilbert
Art Direction: Barbara Scott-Goodman
Production: Kaija Markoe